How to Start a Business and Accounting

The Steps to Starting a Small Business, Creating a Business Plan, Scaling and Hiring along with Basic Accounting Principles

Contents

Part 1: How to Start a Business An Essential Guide to Starting a Small Business from Scratch and Going from Business Idea and Plan to Scaling Up and Hiring Employees

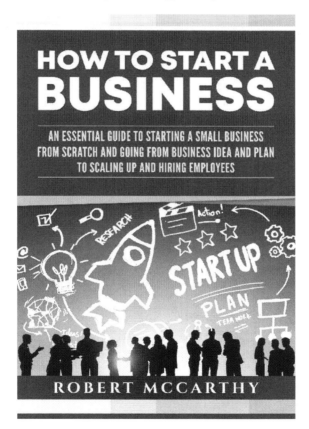

Introduction

Nearly all modern startups are made on a whim.

Entrepreneurship is now becoming a recurrent phenomenon among youth looking to reinvent the future. It's not uncommon to hear of ambitious youth completely heedless of boundaries and filled with remarkable enthusiasm, deciding to start a business in the comfort of their dorm and in the trust-worthy company of future co-founders.

Oftentimes, an idea comes to mind when entrepreneurs run into a problem they cannot immediately overcome. That's when they come up with a solution themselves, and the solution becomes a million-dollar idea for a business. The idea eventually booms into a business and experiences early success. It's rise to glory is plastered all over the news and inspires millions of people.

And that's where the problem comes in.

The simplistic and overly-generic explanation of an entrepreneur's success leaves many optimists thinking that all starting a business takes is an idea. But the business world has never been completely reliant on just creativity – in fact, many successful businesses lack in that area, but do just fine.

Possibly the most common underlying cause of startup failure is lack of a good strategy (which is usually comprised of far more tedious details than innovative ideas). That's not to say that innovation is irrelevant to the success of a business, but no fledgling business can operate without a realistic plan that assesses the number of potential customers it can bring during its infant stages – enough to get the company to stand on its own feet.

Young entrepreneurs are exposed to a plethora of success stories in magazines and blockbuster movies that emphasize the importance of perseverance and a flair for rebellion against the current norm. Those traits may contribute to success, but the stories often leave out the mundane procedures that ground businesses and make them last more than a few years.

You don't come across a news piece about the accountant that did more than prepare reports good enough to survive a surprise audit. Nor do you hear of what type of contract was signed to prevent a founder from being stuck with a partner who nearly destroyed company finances with poor management. That said, it's unlikely management is brought up at all. This reduces the complex equation of business politics and arrangements into this abstract notion of hard work and perseverance.

But that isn't to say that starting a business is all that challenging; it's probably easier than you think, if you know what you're doing and take the time to familiarize yourself with the dull intricacies alongside the more pleasant stages of innovation.

The trick is to know exactly what you're in for before you step into the game. You don't start by introducing your idea to an investor before taking the time to learn about the processes for which you and your potential partners must prepare. Model implementation and product definition must of necessity lead to the less-fun stages of paperwork and financing.

While starting a business has risks, it's never a gamble; it's a process that can be taught, and that's what this book aims to do. Don't think of yourself as an entrepreneur who's about to test their luck with a game of fortune. It's quite likely that your product or service has a demographic somewhere, and all it takes is for you to get a grasp on how to reach your target market efficiently.

With that said, it's best to get some facts and myths out of the way before we delve further into this book; let's strip down the Hollywood/tabloid images of entrepreneurship that may fog your journey to success.

Startups do not mean product-making in a dimly-lit garage. No matter where you decide to develop your idea, you need to understand than starting your company takes more than just a definition of your product. With a new and innovative product comes an equally innovative method to manage it. You are not just building a product, but an institution that can sell your product to the right people.

It's also not a matter of finalizing your idea and introducing it to the public. To up your chances of success, your product needs to be experimented on and introduced to a small group of users that will give you honest feedback. The process of starting a business isn't just a method of making a living and revolutionizing the industry; it's also a process of learning from your users how to render your idea into a product that will be appealing to your customers.

This doesn't mean you have to tailor your product to the opinions of the test- group – at least, not in the exact manner they ask. You could be told that your service or product is faulty due to a particular aspect, but sometimes those who test your product will perceive a unique aspect as a flaw when it's only misunderstood and needs to be better explained.

Lastly, you need to understand that innovation doesn't just boil down to business models and product features. You're going to have to innovate in other areas, like financing, being able to measure your progress, and gauging the potential scale of your success.

And because we want to help you build a solid plan that you can confidently follow, our guide will help you recognize indicators of early success and make sure you don't get caught up in the excitement of developing an idea to the point that you forget to get a handle on rendering it a useful tool to the public.

Techniques and advice in this book are based on real methods that successful startups have used. They will allow you to skip the methodologies which are more likely to fail, and get straight to those that are nearly guaranteed to get you through the phase of "starting up" and into that of implementing and launching.

Chapter One: Initial Idea

Starting and running a business requires courage, drive, and, of course, a lot of planning. If you are reading this, you surely possess the former two because this is a serious business (pun intended). The thought of starting a company has crossed almost everyone's mind, but only a handful put in the time, effort, and hard work required in the planning stage.

This chapter will cover all the aspects of coming up with your business idea (or the practicality of one you already have). It will give you insights and assurance about your concept before you go ahead with it. After all, your idea is the foundation and character of your business.

Asking questions about yourself and your convictions, being convinced about your idea, planning it, and analyzing it practically are the first few steps you can take to frame this essential primary stage.

Question and Evaluate Yourself

If you are determined enough to begin, you need first to question yourself as to why you want to start a business. The answer needs to be more than escaping a routine nine-to-five job, and it should be honest because you need to work with it for the rest of your life. Questioning yourself will diminish the failure probability of your business because you will know whether you can stick to it long-term and put in all the exhausting work to get it to the top.

Questions like...

- Why exactly do you want to open a business when you know the efforts, capital, and time it will require? Is it because you want to be your own boss, or solely because of the financial rewards you would get?
- Do you have enough capital to manage the initial costs?
- If you are working a stable job, are you willing to take the risk of quitting, and put all your time and effort into establishing your business?
- Do you already have an idea for your business? Why would you like to follow that particular concept?
- Are you able to handle pressure in a stressful environment?
- Will you be okay without a helping hand? Can you find solutions to problems on your own? Can you make quick decisions?
- Are you proficient enough to manage a team and give instructions?
- What outcomes do you expect from your business?
- Where do you see yourself and your company in the next five years?
- Are you willing to follow your formulated plan to reach that point?

- Is your objective solely to earn money, or do you also want to develop and learn along the way?

- Have you considered the circumstances in case you fail? Will you be formulating a back-up plan for that possibility?

If you are completely honest with yourself, this checklist will help you determine whether running a business would be a disaster or a piece of cake for you. You can also make a pros-and-cons list to detect your strengths and weaknesses. If you feel that your weaknesses won't drastically affect your work, you can work on them along the way. For example, if you are unable to give proper instructions to your team, you can hire a team head or manager who can direct them, helping you learn this skill while working with them.

Evaluating yourself will give you a translucent glimpse of how well you will manage your business. If you are finding excuses for not starting your own business, it simply means that you aren't confident enough to begin. Perhaps you think the economy is in too bad a shape to start a business? There's never a "bad season" to start a business. In fact, running a company during economic downturns can eliminate competition, thus increasing the demand for your services. You can capture more clients when they have fewer options from which to choose. Also, depending on your type of business, you can have the added benefit of purchasing tools and equipment at lower prices. See, there's always a brighter side to any issue.

This exercise of listing your fears or problems and finding solutions to each can help you gain more confidence and prepare you for the worst. You need to talk to people who are already established within your discipline and are willing to help. Conduct a thorough market analysis as well; we'll talk about that in detail later.

Contemplate Your Business Idea and Concept

To begin, you need an idea, a solid concept. More importantly, you need to reason out why you would like to get into that particular niche.

If you already have an idea in mind and are determined to follow it, there's no point in waiting; it only makes sense to follow through and move on to the next steps.

But if you don't have a concept yet, there's no need to worry. Here are a few ways to help you to generate your big business idea; these tips will also help you elevate your idea if you are already fixed on one.

Dig into Your Skills and Interests

Your personal interests, hobbies, or skills can turn into great business ideas; not only will you get your business running much more passionately, but you will also thoroughly enjoy your work. Make a list of all your interests in one column and your skills in the other. They do not have to be remarkable; it's alright to possess a weird interest or skill if it's one that keeps you captivated. Rank them according to your preference, keeping the business aspect in mind. Match up any interests and skills that go hand-in-hand or complement each other. Skill-and-interest combinations can make for exceptional business concepts. For instance, your interest in food and your baking skills combined could lead you to run a patisserie or a café. If you are skilled in art and adore stationery, you could start a stationery subscription box that reaches out to potential artists every month.

A business concept generated out of your interests and hobbies creates the drive to work hard and put in more effort; moreover, you will earn money from it. As they say, "Turn your hobby into a profession, and you will never have to work." Doing something that grasps your interest creates the benefit of extra care put into the work.; you will never lack motivation, push yourself more to make a difference, and be identified as a passionate entrepreneur that is changing the world one step at a time.

Think About Problems You Face Everyday

Issues in your personal life, business, and personality can also be a source of ideas. For instance, there might be things that you dislike or are unmanageable in your daily life such as the inconvenience of traveling to work, not being able to manage daily cooking and weekly grocery-shopping, struggling with crappy internet, or seeing a flat tire on your car. Solutions: an affordable cab service, a grocery/food delivery app that gets you healthy inexpensive meals, a reliable internet connection service, and a car repair service that can send a nearby mechanic to change the tire. There you have four potential ideas from four everyday problems.

'Think more positively' is a motto to abide by at this stage. Rest assured that you are not the only one dealing with such issues; millions of other working-class people are seeking solutions to such annoyances and are willing to pay in return for additional help that can make their lives easier. Talk to people; list the problems they face in their personal and business lives, compare notes, and you will find potential business ideas right under your nose.

If you are aiming towards solving a problem rather than just earning money, your audience will grow rapidly; if you are selling a product that is needed rather than wanted, you already have their attention. Presenting a solution to a problem that needs immediate attention will turn your business into something that matters to the general public.

Look for Disciplines That Are in Demand

It is also feasible to choose an idea based on recent demands in certain product or service markets, which can make your business an overnight success. If you are not among those who want to find a niche based on their skills, you need to research the latest appeals. For example, fashion is not your forte, but opening an online fashion store with all the best brands can gain traction quickly in the teens-to-young-adults market.

This is another reason why people fear beginning a business; they feel it means inventing something or being the pioneer in their arena. Yes, standing out does matter, but it's not worth dumping a good plan due to the absence of a newly created gimmick. You can smartly pick your niche by searching for high-demand and low-supply fields.

Ask yourself, "How can I make it better?" or "Is there a potential sub-category that can be added to this venue?" Make sure you have done thorough homework about the idea because there might be sensible reasons why there are only a few established companies in a high-demand market. Perhaps the problems are solvable but require a lot of effort which few are willing to make.

If you need to learn a new skill, enroll yourself in a course; if you need to gather huge capital, borrow or take a loan. Just make it happen. You will be extremely grateful and satisfied in the long run to have put in all the effort to push your company to success.

If the constraints seem almost impossible to overcome, solicit professional help. If you have tried your best but cannot make it happen, you might have to rethink that particular idea.

Find Inspiration

There are significant factors within your surroundings that go unnoticed by most. You need to pay attention and constantly observe to find an inspiration that will completely change the game. It could hit you anywhere, in the oddest ways; in a park, in your kitchen, scrolling through social media, or even on the toilet. Seeing the people jogging in the park, concerned about their health and fitness might inspire you to open a fitness center or hire a yoga instructor for your gym; looking at piled-up garbage might lead to you an idea for reducing waste by opening a package-free service which will reduce waste and plastic.

This unconventional method of searching for an idea is not only useful for the beginners but also for those who are fixed on an idea or are already running a stable business. Adding more products or subcategories to your venue can promote your business and help it gain a new identity. Also, tweaking your existing services and reframing them can bring you more clients. Keep an eye out for what people want and what they would like.

Travel can produce business ideas. It's not feasible to travel all the time to find inspiration and ideas; we are just suggesting you take advantage of any opportunity to travel when you get it. You will get to learn about new people, cultures, and ways of living. Suppose you take a trip to Japan and get completely fascinated with the food and culture. You could come back home and research potential business ideas in the area of Japanese food and culture. You could end up opening a ramen and matcha food truck, import Japanese goods and sell them online, or get inspired by traditional Japanese clothing and design a sub-category in your already-established fashion store. The possibilities are endless.

Reading books is another way to travel; it increases knowledge and directs you onto new paths. Flipping through magazines or browsing the internet can lead to brain-storming sessions that lead to an idea. Think, contemplate, come up with an idea or improvement, and stick to it.

Market Research

Once you are content with your idea and excited to start following it, you need to analyze it by conducting market analysis, research, and surveys, or by seeking advice from fellow business-owners. This step will ensure the viability of your idea.

Say, for instance, your idea is to open a cleaning service. You can run a market analysis on the existing number of cleaning businesses in your area, the percentage of successful or renowned establishments, and their years in business. List and compare their service types, their hourly or per-square-foot rate patterns, hours of operation, types of clientele, and other criteria. This will help you chart out the success rate of that type of business in your area and indicate your chances of a favorable outcome.

This applies to any idea; research the competition within your niche. Doing this will also help you to frame a business model for your services, such as lashing down rates, providing promotional codes and coupons, developing an application, or coming up with additional perks that can attract customers. It will not only bring you more customers initially but also authorize your name in the market. The idea is to stand out; people need to be confident in hiring you over others because you are different and better.

Again, answering a relevant set of questions for this step can also help you predict how well your business idea will run.

Are you offering different services than others in your vicinity?

- If not, what is the level of competition, and how does your idea stand out?
- Are there feasible ways to make your service better?
- Who will be your target audience?
- How will you make your company more accessible to your customers?

- Will your clientele willingly pay for your services?
- Will your investment receive substantial returns within an ideal time period?

As we said, it's okay not to have a completely distinctive idea if your approach is to make amendments and changes that will make your product or service stand out. A proper business plan can serve to merely adorn your idea, which we'll talk more about it later.

Another important aspect to consider is your target audience, and how easily they can access your services. You need to analyze whether your clientele is more open to technology and website usage or to speaking on a phone. If you are targeting the younger audience, say between 20 to 35 years, your services would be more accessible through a website. If your audience is older, phone calls or scheduling meetings is better for them. Surveys and statistics based on the reachability of your service can help you develop your idea accordingly.

Fixing your rates in a smart manner is also essential in the starting stage because your products or services are not tested by any of your clients yet, and so there is no proof of how genuine and good they are. You might want to strategize your prices according to the current market value to gain more clients in the beginning. If you provide top-notch services, they are bound to come back and spread the word.

Next, work out an analysis of the capital you will invest in your idea and the probable return on the investment. Take the help of financial advisors to determine the income and cash flow, and the anticipated time period of the initial cost. We will talk more about the finances, running rates, and capital part of your business in the following chapters of this book.

Most importantly, build an excellent network that can educate you about things of which you may have been completely unaware. Since you are new to running a business, guidance and insights from experts can be invaluable in helping you learn better ways to handle problems and meet the needs of your customers. You will learn the secret behind the mantra, "Work smarter, not harder."

No business idea is too big or too small. If you have what it takes and are ready to put in what is required, you can turn a small and insignificant idea into a revenue-generating machine. Above all, question yourself; be honest, trust your instincts, gather courage, be practical and confident, believe in yourself, and unravel your potential. You've got this.

In the coming chapters, you will learn how to push your business idea forward by forming a business plan, engaging the legal procedures, and developing ways to promote your business once it is up-and-running.

Chapter Two: Business Plan

There's a quote known throughout the world of business:

"If you fail to plan, you plan to fail."

Your business plan can be the single most important factor that determines how successful your business is going to be. If you think this an exaggeration, wait until the end of this chapter and think again.

So, if it's such an important thing, what exactly is a business plan? Let's get right into it.

What Is a Business Plan and Why Is It Important?

Your business plan covers every aspect of your business; it includes everything from why you're thinking about creating this business to the opportunity you found in the market to the market analysis, marketing strategy, financial plan, your business structure, and everything in between and beyond.

Creating a business plan is the most critical thing you need to do right away, for three good reasons.

The first reason is that your business plan is going to act as your road map. It will be the guide that you'll religiously follow in every step of your business, from research and development to launching your business and hiring your team. The more effort and detail you put into it, the clearer and more reliable your plan will be.

The second reason is that if you have no idea what to write in your plan just yet, then this is when you *most* need to devise your business plan. You don't have to know everything; once you start on your plan, you'll find that there are way too many aspects of the business you're trying to create that you had no idea you should even consider. You'll be forced to start looking beyond what you know. Not only will you gain invaluable insights into how to properly launch your business but you'll also question your initial idea, examine different practices in the market, and start on more solid ground.

Finally, the third reason is that once you start the operations of your business, you'll inevitably lose focus on (or entirely forget) many of the finer details - unless you have everything on paper. And having your thoughts on paper is completely different from having a perfectly written and well-articulated plan at your disposal. This plan will not only act as your guide and a reminder of important details but ll also serve as the proof of your conscientious preparation to present to investors, potential partners, and others in other kinds of business relations.

Before Starting Your Business Plan

Before getting started on your plan, there a few things that you should do first.

Widen Your Scope with Research

Research is going to be your best companion on the journey of devising your plan. You're going to research your business idea, the businesses you'll be competing with, your marketing strategy, your target audience - and you'll have to look through a lot of statistics, best practices, and advice. Whatever you know, your research will fortify it or present you with better alternatives. Whatever you don't know, you'll get to know through research. We can't stress how important research is!

Decide Why You're Writing this Plan

There are many reasons to write a business plan, and you need to define yours. Are you seeking investment? If so, what kind of investors are you targeting, and in what aspects will they be most interested? You'll want to give them everything they need, without beating around the bush too much. Are you creating this plan for your team members, so that they can have a clearer idea of their role? Do you need this business plan for your own sake, as your road map and reference manual? The reason you're writing the business will guide your research and the road you take in creating the plan.

Be Detailed, but Avoid Exaggerating Your Plan

The more detailed the plan, the better. However, there's a difference between attention to details and redundant over-use of information. Your business plan should include all the important aspects of your business, in much detail; after all, it *is* your road map. But once you start cramming in information for the sake of increasing the number of your pages, you're just wasting time. Remember, you don't have to write a 100-page plan. A solid, bulletproof, backed-up plan of 10 pages can prove to be much more useful than a 100-page plan that gets you lost every time you look at it.

Research Business Plans and Choose One

When it comes to creating a business plan, there are different schools of thought. Many startups choose to go with a lean start-up plan, using the Business Model Canvas (BMC) or its even leaner "modified version". Others go for traditional business templates that are more detailed. You can choose either form to get started, but sooner or later, you'll figure out that both methods complement each other. We recommend that you start with a BMC and then devise your detailed business plan.

Creating Your Business Model Canvas

A BMC contains nine key elements:

Key Partnerships

In this section, you list all the partners that will be essential for the operations of your business; your strategic partners, which include manufacturers, suppliers, contractors, and others. You'll also list why they'd be interested in partnering up with you.

Key Activities

What kind of activities does your business rely on in its operation? These are the activities that reflect your value proposition, your vision, and your goals. They're also the activities that will benefit your business in its competitive advantage over others.

Value Proposition

Why is your business important? Why should it be out in the market? What need does it fill, or what opportunity does it serve? Your value proposition is the core value your business provides to its customers.

Customer Relationship

How will you be contacting your customers? How will they contact you? Will your business be automated online, will you deal with them physically, or is a mix of both? Is that how your target segment expects your customer relationship to be, or do they prefer other alternatives?

Customer Segment

Whom will you be targeting with your products and services? Are they men, women, or both? Are you targeting adults, kids, or parents? Which class are you targeting? If you're targeting more than one segment, then which is your most important customer?

Key Resources

These are the resources you'll need to use to create value for your customers. Your key resources can include capital, team members, equipment, or even intellectual property.

Distribution Channels

How will you reach your customers? Do you have a physical product that needs to be shipped? Do you have a customer-service department that keeps in contact with your customers? If so, then how does the communication work? Which are the most effective channels, how much do they cost, and how do they fit into your operational plan?

Cost Structure

This section includes details about the ongoing costs of running your business, including daily operational costs, payroll, periodical subscriptions, and any other recurrent costs. Next, you'll pinpoint the most expensive resources and/or activities; from there you can decide whether you want to focus on cutting down costs or improving value.

Revenue Stream

Arguably the most important aspect of any business is: how will you make money? What values do you provide that your customers will be willing to pay for? How will they pay? There can be more than more one revenue stream and different strategies for profit, all of which you should list here.

Your Business Plan: A Step-By-Step Guide

Moving on to your business plan, here are the most essential elements in any business plan:

Executive Summary

Your executive summary is the most important part of your plan. It should be the first thing that any potential lenders or investors see, but it's the part that you're going to write after you finish up all the other parts of your plan.

Your executive summary should convey your passion, goals, vision, and the most important aspects of your plan. Anyone reading it should feel excited about reading the rest of the plan; if they're not, there's a problem.

Typically, your executive summary will include the following:

- A brief introduction to your business; essentially a description of your company (its Vision and Mission Statement), its key products and/or services, and your goals in creating this business
- Your target market(s)
- Your competitive advantage
- An overview of your team and its qualifications
- A financial outlook that describes the capital you need, how you'll utilize it, and how you'll turn it into profits.

Company Description

Your company description includes the following points:

Mission Statement

What's the main value and purpose of your business? It shouldn't take more than one or two sentences.

Vision

Where do you see this business going after "x" number of years? What are your aspirations, and what's the next level of this business?

Goals

Here you'll list both your long-term and short-term goals. These should be realistic yet challenging goals. You'll also describe how you'll measure your performance using KPIs and your milestones.

Target Market

While you'll get into your target market in detail in the marketing plan section, an overview of your target market and its unique characteristics goes here.

Industry

What's the industry you're getting into, and what's its current state? Is it expanding, mature, or stable? What are the speculations for this industry in the short and long runs? Are there any gaps or opportunities you're utilizing? How are your competitors in this industry doing, and what's your edge over them?

Legal Structure

What kind of business will you be running? Will it be a sole proprietorship, an LLC, partnership, or corporation? Do you have any partners or investors holding some of your shares? How are the shares divided?

Products and Services

In this section you'll get into the details regarding your products and/or services. You should include the following:

1. A detailed description of your products and/or services. If there are any technical specification documents, attach them to the Appendices.

2. What problems do they solve? Explain in detail their benefits, features, and competitive advantage over similar products and services.

3. Are there any proprietary features backing up your competitive edge? This can be a patent, a license, or an exclusive agreement with one of your strategic partners that none of your competitors have.

4. What's the pricing strategy for your products and services? Will it be based on subscription, on one-time-pay, fees, or a lease? How does your pricing stand among the competition? What's your profit margin?

Marketing Plan

Your marketing plan covers the details about the industry, your competition, your target market, and your marketing strategy. You need to start with the following:

Market Research

In your market research, you'll get your information from two sources: data that you collect yourself, and the available data in journals, research articles, and trusted whitepapers. Through your research, you should acquire the following information:

What's the total size of your industry?

What's the industry outlook? Is it expanding or diminishing?

The total size of your target market in the industry

Realistically speaking, how much of this target market can you reach and/or dominate?

What are the trends in your target market? What will your customers expect from you?

Obstacles

Are there any obstacles that will come in the way of your entering the market? How do you plan on overcoming them? These obstacles can be:

- High costs of starting up, production, marketing, or operation

- Strong competition

- Hiring employees of sufficient qualifications on a limited budget

Threats and Opportunities

Once you have a solid plan to overcome the barriers, what are the challenges you're going to face once you're in the industry? What are the opportunities you can use for your benefit? It's common to perform a SWOT analysis in this section of the plan.

Target Customers

You'll get into your target customers in detail in this part. You'll divide them into "user personas", listing the distinguishing characteristics of each one, their behaviors, and what would attract them to your products/services

Key Competitors

You've already given an overview of your competitors, and now it's time to get into more detail. You'll create a detailed competitor's data collection plan in which you'll include:

- Their prices

- Their benefits and features

- How profitable and scalable their business is

- Their marketing strategy

Next, you'll use this data to compare where you stand to them in a competitive analysis worksheet. This is where you list all your marketing aspects and compare it to theirs, ranking your performance to get a clear idea of where you stand in the market.

Positioning

Once you're clear about your industry, threats, opportunities, target customers, and key competitors, you should know how you'll position your business in the market using your competitive advantage.

Marketing Strategy

Your marketing strategy will include the online and offline portals you're going to use. If you focus on online marketing, you'll need to include the platforms you'll use, your content marketing strategy, your promotional strategy, and your PR plan.

Operational Plan

Your operational plan should give the reader a clear idea about your business's daily operations. To do that, you'll describe:

Production & Quality Control

What are the methods you'll use to produce a physical product or deliver an intangible service? If there are any equipment and/or technology costs, you should specify them in detail. You should also describe your plan on how you'll provide consistent quality in your products and services.

Location

If your business has a physical address, you should specify it in detail. This includes its complete address, the size of your office, the type of building, accessibility, facility costs, and utilities.

Legal Environment

Are there any legal requirements you should handle? These can include licenses, permits, insurance coverage, regulations, copyrights, or bonding.

Personnel

What kind of personnel will be working on your team? Will you hire full or part-timers? Freelancers or contractors? What's the job description, qualifications, and compensation of each? How will you find your team, and what sort of training will they need?

Other Operations

If your business depends on other operations, such as inventory maintenance, suppliers, or distribution channels, you should specify them in detail.

Management and Organization

This is where you describe the roles of everyone in your business. In describing your management team, you should include the following:

- Their biographies
- How you'll cover any gaps in the management structure
- Your business advisors
- An organizational chart

Expenses and Capitalization

These are the expenses you'll need to for launching. It doesn't include your daily finances, those will be included in your financial plan. For this section, you'll describe the following in detail:

- Your startup expenses
- Your launching day expenses

- Personal financial statement

Financial Plan

Your financial plan will cover in detail your daily expenses, projecting, in turn, your profit and growth over specified periods. In your financial plan, you'll discuss the following:

- Projection of profits and losses in first twelve months after startup

- A speculated balance sheet about the financial state of your business one year after launching

- An operational plan of three years that speculates your profits and losses

- The details of your cash flow at any given time

Appendices

You'll find that, across your plan, there are many detailed documents that serve the purpose of the section you're working on. However, whoever is reading your plan will most likely want to get an overview at first without getting into too many technical details. For this purpose, you'll include these documents in your Appendices.

Refining the Plan

Depending on the purpose of your plan, you might want to refine it to match whoever will be reading it. As we've mentioned previously, an investor will be looking for certain financial and strategic aspects of your business, but they might not want to know whether you intend to hire full-time employers or freelancers. Once you've finalized your plan, you'll be able to refine it to better match your purpose, maybe even create different versions for different targets.

Business Plans Best Practices

When it comes to business plans, there are way too many. They differ in many aspects, from the elements discussed to their layouts and styles of presentation. Here are some of the best practices when it comes to creating a business plan:

Data Visualization and Organization

If you look at this marketing strategy created by Nivea for Men, you'll find that they've used a simple diagram to convey their tactics.

Other forms of data visualization and organization can include diagrams, charts, and tables.

Trustworthy Resources

Sometimes getting accurate information can be difficult, no matter how much your business depends on the accuracy of this information. This is something that the managers at Airport Cafe were able to find their way around when they wanted to open a new branch in another terminal. They collected the data they needed about passengers and their behavior directly from the Airport Authorities, which allowed them to create a correct estimation in their business plan.

Concise Yet Comprehensive Information

A long business plan is not always the best; if you're able to address your key points in a shorter one, that will probably be best. This is a fictional concise-yet-comprehensive plan that serves its purpose:

How All Great Businesses Have Bulletproof Plans

If you're still having second thoughts about the importance of business plans, then perhaps you need to look at any of the successful businesses operating today and research their startup. They didn't start with getting finances, they didn't hire their team members first, and they most certainly didn't start with pitching their business idea. Their work started long before anyone had ever heard of them. It all started with a plan, a plan about what to do long before their business was ready to go out into the light, and a plan covering what they needed to do once their business was launched.

And yet, many people spend extraordinary amounts of time and effort creating a business plan, only to become discouraged and give up on their dream altogether. The reason is usually that when it finally comes time for execution, their business plan isn't executable; it isn't realistic. That shouldn't make you think that business plans are worthless; on the contrary, it should encourage you to bulletproof your plan.

The way great businesses bridge the gap between a business plan on paper and a successful real-life business is by putting everything they know on paper. Next, they research, talk to mentors, listen to the stories of those who've walked this path before, and then re-evaluate their plan. Perhaps the most important aspect of creating a bulletproof plan is, well, to bulletproof it. That can only happen by letting yourself go as far and high with your imagination, dreams, and aspirations as you want - and then grounding your plan with down-to-earth bulletproofing.

Chapter Three: Finances Sorted

Starting and running a business both require capital, which is often difficult to acquire. A crucial step towards a successful business involves birthing the finances for its operation. Anyone who has a great business idea and a plan to develop it can fall back when it comes to the financial aspect. Basic questions like, "How much will it cost me? Will I be able to gather enough capital? What if my plan backfires and I end up losing all my money?" are off-putting.

It is a big risk to put in a huge amount of money with the uncertainty of getting it back. But if you possess the drive and passion for getting your business where it deserves to be, you are bound to get the return of your investment and more. You just need a plan and a straight mind to set it up, which is what this book is about.

Getting your finances in order can be a complicated process, especially when you have just stepped into the business world. To ease the stress, we have divided this stage into various categories to help you understand all aspects in depth.

Let's begin by talking about the primary financial aspect of your funding plan: startup capital.

What is Startup Capital?

To earn money, you need money. It's the pragmatic truth behind every business. A company would require a certain amount of funding to begin running, which is known as startup funding or startup capital. This might include basic costs from purchasing equipment for your business to covering employee salaries and paying taxes.

There are certain varying terminologies depending on the type of capital you are approaching. For instance, the term seed capital refers to the funding required for planning and researching your idea before you finalize it. Startup capital is the funding required for the basic costs before launching, such as workspace rent and setup.

The next type is expansion capital, also known as mezzanine capital, which takes your company to a higher level and funds the improvements made for its growth.

There are a lot of ways to gather funding for your business, which we will cover in further detail. To understand it in a basic sense, capital is categorized as one of two types: debt capital and equity capital.

Debt Capital

This label applies to the capital borrowed either through banks or in the form of loans from relatives or lenders with interest rates and fees. Even though it takes a while to pay back the full amount with the additional costs, you would still be the sole owner of the company without sharing any equity or partnership.

Equity Capital

Equity capital is when an investor or a bigger company agrees to fund your business when it is in its initial stage in exchange for a certain percentage of the company's profits. It gives them the benefit of profiting from it when the business has grown and is running successfully. Even though you are relieved from repaying the loan amount, there is the forfeit of a stake in your company, affecting its functioning and negating sole ownership.

Funding Your Business – The Options

While there are multiple funding options, each comes with a set of benefits and risks. You need to weigh them out and decide on the most sensible one, or elect more than one option and garner funding from two or three sources, which could help reduce the risks of losing everything at once and provide a back-up plan in case of failure of one source.

A few finance options to fund your business are:

Savings or Self-Financing

The first plan would be to self-finance your business; it is relatively easy and less of a procedure to convert your personal assets into business capital. Having a personal investment in your business shows your commitment to the enterprise, which is a strong selling point for potential investors and business partners; it will not only get your business running sooner but could also attract extra funding.

There is a big downside to putting in a personal investment. If your business fails, you will end up losing everything, which will have a huge impact on your life. The fear of this may well provide you the motivation to work harder and make sure your business succeeds; if it does, you will recoup your investment and realize some profit that much earlier.

Taking a Loan

When you want to avoid the risk of losing all your savings and ending up nowhere, your backup plan would be taking a bank loan. It is, however, a nerve-wracking procedure given the amount of data and papers it requires. Moreover, the interest charged is anywhere from 6% to 14%, which adds up to a huge sum at the end. Getting a loan is not easy, because you're required to present either collateral of equivalent value to the mortgage it or an amazing credit score. A poor credit score/history means lessened odds of getting a loan, but there are banks and lenders who charge a higher interest rate while lending a small principal amount to the poor credit-score holders.

Another popular option is to enlist a co-signer on a loan; the co-signer can be a friend or relative who has a good credit score. In case of failure to repay, the bank will seek out the co-signer, so consider the implications if using this option.

Search for various lenders, talk to them, compare their services and interest rates, and go for the best.

Crowdfunding

Having recently gained considerable traction, crowdfunding is a popular choice among start-up companies who have their marketing strategies and product display ready to show to their audience. There are a lot of websites now which encourage and support crowdfunding. It is basically a platform where companies that have insufficient funds but a great idea pitch their concept to the general audience and request small contributions from the greatest possible number of them. It is sometimes accompanied by promises of discounted or free merchandise once the company is running.

These crowdfunding websites market themselves, so having your concept presented on them is a viable tool for attracting potential clients as well as investors. They will definitely cut themselves a small percentage of the gathered fund; however, be advised that if the crowd-funding website fails to collect the total anticipated amount, you do not get anything, and the money is returned to the respective donors. So, to receive large donations from a lot of individuals, you need to present a promising concept displayed impressively. Use creative ways to do so, like an animated video, a podcast, or a detailed presentation of your long-term goals.

Angel Investors

Angel investors are usually past owners of a successful business, or simply rich individuals who have a penchant for business and are ready to invest in potential business ideas. These angel investors often like to be a part of the company's accounting and management department, or an active member of the board of directors, using their control of the background activities to be more informed.

You don't need to have personal contacts to search for an angel investor. There are organizations that have advisory relationships with numerous angel investors that could support your business if intrigued by its concept.

Venture Capital

Also known as VC, Venture Capital firms look for start-up companies with stellar growth potential, or, sometimes, companies already established, and generally in the computer or high-tech fields. Venture capitalists invest a huge amount of capital in businesses, expecting to gain equity stakes from their investments along with selling them as an IPO (initial public offering) or to other established businesses.

Venture Capital investment can provide significant capital for your business if it requires large funding, but the results delivered need to be exceptional. Venture capitalists expect not only a return of investment but also huge profits from your promising idea.

Borrowing from Friends and Family

If you want to avoid selling stakes from your business or paying usurious interest, borrowing money from your friends and family may be a viable option. Your family and friends understand that it takes time to build a business and that profits usually start coming in only after a few years; they might be inclined to give you a generous amount of time to return the borrowed money.

You might want to consider the risks of ruining relationships that come with this option. It would be difficult to pay them back in case your business fails, weakening their trust in you. At times, a few practical thinkers might want some kind of equity in your business as well, raising the chance of increasing complications between you. So, think twice before considering this option. It might be the easiest but it also comes with the most emotional risk.

Other Financing Options

Credit cards are another way to cover your initial expenses. The amount of money you borrow comes with a huge interest rate at the end of each month, which can get daunting. If you have used a credit card before, you probably know how quickly the interest adds up in case you neglect to repay in full. Certain credit-card deals, however, are tailored to meet business funding demands, providing cash-back and other attractive options.

Business incubators are an attractive option to receive additional services and advice, along with capital funding. They provide resources, tools, technical assistance, and/or marketing to save a new business money until the company can move into its own premises. Often, universities or some government organizations act as business incubators to benefit from the product development, marking them as an important section of the business forever. There are a few downsides to seeking a business incubator, such as going through a long procedure to get in, and higher chances of being rejected if there is too much competition or if your idea is not promising enough to succeed.

And then, there are **online peer-to-peer ("P2P") loan organizations** that lend money to small businesses with a straightforward approach unlike banks. You just fill in your request for funding and your business outline, and the website helps you receive the total fund from a pool of investors. You then need to repay the platform in monthly installments which go back to the investors. It also gives you lower interest rates and higher chances of approval. However, you need to have a good credit score to be considered for receiving funding. This approach of benefiting from P2P platforms is increasingly popular due to its ease of use and higher success rates.

If you have already sorted out the funding for your business's startup, there are further aspects that need to be managed while starting your company.

Budgeting and Upfront Costs

To start a business, a few basic costs are absolutely necessary and unavoidable. You need to budget to cover all costs for the first two to three years of starting your business. Forget about earning profit within this period. You need to solely focus on running the company smoothly without financial stress.

A few things to keep in mind while budgeting your start-up finances are:

• Calculating the basic upfront costs required to start any kind of business. We have a checklist here which will help in managing those.

1. License and Registration Fees
2. Equipment and Tools such as computers, printers, billing machines, furniture, etc.
3. Office and Workspace Costs such as monthly rents or renovations
4. Insurance
5. Taxes
6. Employee Salaries
7. Product Development (depending on your business type)
8. Marketing and Advertising
9. Inventory
10. Website and Application Development

11. Utilities and Office Supplies

12. Miscellaneous costs such as hiring consultants, travel, or shipping

• Coming up with a realistic figure of how much money you can spend each month and dividing the costs accordingly, depending on the monthly expense and sales.

• Setting the total amount of funding you would require after these calculations and estimating the time duration you would need it for. Make sure to increase and decrease your sales graph calculations depending on the seasonal demand. Often, companies need a few years to get to the break-even point, and thus, a realistic time period would give you the chance of repaying the total investment amount within the promised time.

• Overestimating the budget and keeping an emergency fund on the side can help you cover unexpected costs such as equipment damage or covering employee salaries during sales lulls.

• Once you have your required amount along with the emergency fund, arranging for the total a few months in advance. Even if you are aiming to receive the needed amount through various options at once, approach them at the same time and make efforts to receive them all at once. This will let you start your company at a smoother pace.

Where Can You Cut Costs?

Money saved is money earned. Cutting costs while starting a business can help in saving a lot of money in unimaginable ways. These are a few tips through which you can cut costs:

> • Look for numerous insurance policies and land on one which is cost-effective

- Reduce travel costs by conducting virtual meetings and interviews. It will also save you a lot of time which can be put into something more productive.

- Try purchasing supplies and utilities in bulk instead of smaller quantities. Buying them in bulk can get you a wholesale price instead of retail.

- If you have a basement or a warehouse that's been locked up and unused for a while, you can renovate it and use it as an office space. It will save you from paying rent every month, which is a major expense.

- If you feel that your workload doesn't require a full-time employee, you can hire fewer staff members and get particular tasks done by freelancers or virtual assistant companies, hence saving monthly salary payments.

Cutting costs to manage finances is an arduous phase in the beginning. However, skimping on necessary aspects, such as avoiding marketing or purchasing low-quality equipment, can affect the functionality of your business.

Common Mistakes and Pitfalls to Avoid

- Never underestimate your startup capital. You can incur unexpected costs at any point. Always overestimate your budget to be assured of meeting your monthly expenses.

- Avoid the mistake of expecting too much too soon. Being extremely optimistic about higher sales and timely payments can lead to improper budgeting of your finances every month. Sometimes, payments are delayed, or sales are decreased due to off-season fluctuations. You should be prepared to absorb the costs when you do not receive the expected returns.

• You cannot leave out your salary. Many entrepreneurs fail to add their own salaries on the balance sheet, even months after establishing their business, as a way of cutting costs. If you feel that your business cannot pay you well enough after a while, what's the point of running it in the first place?

• Do not take too many loans. It will just pile up your debt and affect your credit score in the longer run. If you are taking a loan to pay off the earlier one, you are just adding other fees and interests, making the situation worse for you. Arrange a proper refinancing plan and look for more sensible options to combat this situation.

To sum up the financial aspect of beginning your business, answer the following questions to come up with a rough idea about the direction you want to take:

• Which funding option seems the most feasible for you?

• Do you want to take a loan and repay the full amount within a few years?

• Are you ready to share a percentage of your company with an investor to receive the funding?

• Do you have a proper budgeting plan regarding the dollar amount and the time required to reach the break-even point?

• Can you support yourself until you make a profit?

• Are you ready to face unexpected financial situations? Do you have an emergency funding plan?

• Can you arrange for the total capital requirements well in advance?

Consider these questions honestly and realistically, because financing a business is not child's play. You must be thoroughly prepared and informed and take the leap only when you are fully confident of overcoming any circumstances.

Chapter Four: Finding A Mentor - Learn from the Experience of Others & Know Your Limits

Business publications and entrepreneurship books are great sources of the latest business news and strategies. The authors of these pieces are professionals who started from square one and are able to provide helpful insight to help you evaluate where you stand in your current plan, and how far you are from your goal. However, no matter how resourceful these online sources can be, they can never compare to hands-on mentorship from a business guru who can guide you on an on-going basis until your project is on a firm footing.

In short, a business mentor is a professional business owner who can act as your guide for an extended period, free of charge.

You might wonder why business gurus would want to invest their time and effort on new entrepreneurs if there is no financial compensation. For many of them, it's because they want to give back to their community and help mentees overcome the obstacles that the mentors once faced.

This section will guide you through the steps needed to find the right business mentor for your project, and how to maintain a long-lasting relationship with them that will help you and your business head in the right direction.

Why Get a Mentor?

While this isn't an obligatory step in growing your business, it will certainly accelerate the time taken to see your project boom. When you start your own business, you become your own boss, which can be challenging when you're still a budding entrepreneur. Having a mentor will speed up the sometimes-painful process of learning the intricacies of business implementation and leadership.

Getting Started: Where to Find a Mentor

Educate yourself first

While finding a mentor is an optional step, it's not one that you can leap to; never skip self-teaching. Make it a habit to read business publications and books; feed your own learning process and keep yourself updated on the latest news in commerce. Keep your mind business oriented.

Bear in mind that one day *you* may be the mentor, teaching a mentee who has reached out to you.

Explore local business communities and events

Whether it's a local Chamber of Commerce or informal business meetups in your area, such community events will often have entrepreneurs who are willing to give their insights to attendees. Even better, they will generally welcome being approached by less experienced individuals asking for mentorship

With that said, these kinds of meetups or workshops are a great place to meet *potential* mentors, but that doesn't mean that you should decide whom you want to establish as your coach on a whim. If you meet anyone whom you think can provide you with useful information, ask them anything off the top of your head in the meantime, and request their contact information to formally introduce yourself later and find out where you can meet them again.

Join a startup incubator

Incubators are tailored spaces for young entrepreneurs with limited funds or very few employees. These spaces have resources that help a growing business get started and overcome hurdles by providing a free or affordable workspace alongside access to investors and potential mentors. In some cases, incubators can even offer you capital and/or will recommend the right mentor for your business needs.

But you don't have to follow their recommendations; take time to explore the space and see if you spot any business owners that may provide you with insight into areas where you lack skills or need information. While recommended mentors may be a perfect fit for your business, they may not fit with *your* skills and needs.

Use your own connections

While exploring beyond the parapet of your former connections is an excellent way to broaden your professional network, never underestimate the power of professionals who once inspired you in the past. These could be business owners with whom you crossed paths years ago, or college professors who know the convolutions of the business world best and likely know more about your field of choice than your peers.

If you're unsure how to determine whether a professional could be of help, ask yourself if they have a broad network of business gurus and investors from which to draw their information. Some of them may not have the time to mentor, but others will be willing to provide you with what you need to further your career.

How to Choose a Mentor

Never choose an investor to be your mentor

Your circle of investors and peers are trusted individuals who want your project to succeed as much as you do, and that's exactly why they cannot provide you mentorship. Anyone, including friends or family, who might be emotionally invested in you or your project, should never be those you turn to for critique.

Advice should never be sugarcoated, and sometimes getting feedback will be as harsh as a professional frankly telling you that your business model is not feasible or that it's unlikely to succeed. These are insights that a friend or investor will never be able to perceive because they're typically thinking inside the same box as you.

An ideal business mentor is someone who can see the full picture and whose relationship with you is strictly professional. This doesn't mean that you need someone who will give you nothing but negative feedback, but mentors should be honest and analytical as well as motivating. Quality mentorship should always have a positive effect on entrepreneurs, driving them to dream big and take long shots but through realistic strategies.

Choose a good listener

A professional who doesn't take the time to listen to you and only throws generic advice your way is a bad fit for you, and in most cases, for any other entrepreneur as well. You've already had your share of general How-To's and technical advice from books and business news. What you should be looking for is someone who will answer *your* questions, rather than provide you with a set of generic FAQs.

A good listener will take your personal struggles into account and generously offer advice on each of your inquiries. Some of them will take the time to listen to what you have to say all at one go, in order to analyze your character and see what approaches could work for you.

A mentor should never assume that you will be making the same decisions that they would. Instead, they should think like the best version they believe you could be, rather than the best version of themselves.

Choose a humble mentor

Mentors should never be parental or condescending. Although the latter is uncommon, you'll find yourself running into the former quite often on your hunt for the perfect mentor. A good mentor will treat you as their equal, and not as a child that reminds them of their earlier days. Oddly enough, this is more common among younger successful entrepreneurs who have recently "made it."

A mentor should never treat you like they're your boss; one of the primary reasons you've decided on this journey is to be your own boss. Professionals who make good mentors will offer you advice, not orders. They will recommend trying out certain strategies, but will not assign you homework. Someone who behaves as your superior will gradually cause you to feel dependent on receiving orders, when it's essential for you to feel confident that you can take the wheel once your mentor is no longer in the picture.

Don't be afraid to go big

Do not purposely aim for a smaller target-mentor, assuming that more prestigious business owners will not agree to be your mentor. On the contrary, established companies are *more* likely to have CEOs that dedicate a good chunk of their time to give back to the community.

That doesn't mean that only famous entrepreneurs will have the qualities that render them the quintessential mentor. Even those who run relatively small businesses can be of immense help. If you come across a business that it inspires you, large or small, never hesitate to try to meet the mastermind behind it.

Connecting: How to Set Up Meetings

Make yourself reachable

Once you've met your mentor, you need to make yourself easily accessible to them. Always return their calls and respond to their emails as swiftly as possible. A mentor should never have to chase you for a meeting from which *you* will benefit.

Be frank with your mentor about what you expect

Avoid using the word "mentor" in your first meeting. Even though they probably expect it, you should take the time to connect in those first casual meetings, discussing your common interests and insights in the business world. The first meeting will allow both of you to decide whether the other person is a good fit for a mentoring relationship.

As you follow up with them, you may then bring up your interest in mentorship and regular consultation. If they agree to your proposition and offer a fee, turn it down. An entrepreneur should never have to pay for mentorship.

Invest in your relationship

Once you have established your mentor-mentee relationship, make sure you frequently meet up. The whole purpose of mentorship is to learn what textbooks can't teach you: hands-on experience. It would be a waste of a connection to rely on back-and-forth emails between you and your mentor.

Take them to your workspace or office. Discuss your concerns and any hurdles in the way of your business growth, and introduce your mentor to your personnel, if you have any.

Business Mentorship: What to Expect

Honest feedback

What to expect from your mentor is primarily something that *you* decide, unless your business growth is stunted for reasons that you don't understand or can't pinpoint. If you've picked the right mentor, they will start by offering you an all-encompassing evaluation of your business idea, model, and how effectively you're running your company.

Many entrepreneurs are so emotionally invested in their business models and ideas that they typically reject any critique, and only want a series of crash courses. This will never be the case. Be emotionally prepared for critique and listen to your mentor's advice on how to improve areas that need some work.

A personal approach

A business mentor will confidentially listen to your concerns and analyze everything that worries you about your business. They will not provide you psychiatric counseling, nor will they only give you technical advice. They're not business advisors, they're confidantes. Expect them to share their own stories of failure and how they managed to overcome the drawbacks. They may pinpoint your weaknesses and advise you on how to work on them.

Help you didn't expect

Let's say that the primary reason you consulted a mentor was that you were looking to implement an impeccable sales model. You may find that your mentor will stop you and take you two steps back, to where you missed something more important. They may point out poor time management skills, ask you about your sleeping habits, advise you to give yourself more time off, and provide you with other advice that you least expected.

And even though it may feel like there's no time to slow down, your mentor speaks of experience and knows best when it comes to a healthy working pace. You may think that working upwards of ten hours a day will get you to launch your business faster, but your mentor knows that it will end up burning you out in a matter of weeks, leading to further delay. Listen to your mentor and learn from their failures and experiences.

EQ skills

You can't have a successful business with unhappy employees. Your mentor should teach you to have better control over your own emotions as well as that of your personnel. They will work on making you more self-aware of your weaknesses and strengths. They'll also advise you on how to interact with your employees in a manner that is motivational while maintaining boundaries that will have your personnel seeing you as a supportive superior.

During your mentorship, you should feel your motivation become more grounded in realistic goals. Your mentor will help you understand that while dreaming big is helpful, baby steps should be applied wherever possible.

Mentorship is an efficient way to make sure you're on the right track, but it's not a delegation of responsibilities. A mentee primarily does all the work, while a mentor will find ways around weaknesses, and will make sure that no risky decisions are made without the consequences being pointed out to their mentees.

Remember that you're not taking a shortcut by consulting another professional, but rather, you're learning from the hands-on experience of other business gurus to up your chances of success.

Chapter Five: The Company You Keep - Who Is Going on The Journey with You?

Two heads are better than one when it comes to running a business and finding the right partner for your journey can generate significantly more great ideas and solutions to problems. It's also good security to have someone to rely on in the event you have to opt-out temporarily, while having more shoulders to bear responsibilities.

When it comes to startups, a partner can help lower the costs to launch by providing more capital. You may think that splitting the income sounds less appealing, but in most cases, the benefits outweigh the costs.

But finding the right partner for your startup is a tricky business, and it doesn't just boil down to someone you can trust with your company. Although having a partner can open more doors for your business, you're also looking at twice as many disagreements, legal liabilities, weaknesses, and other changes that may threaten the success of your project.

Before you consider finding a business partner, let's look at how you could avoid a detrimental partnership by considering these areas.

What Makes a Business Partnership Detrimental?

An efficient way to make sure that you don't get caught up in a bad partnership is to know what *makes* a partnership bad. These are some of the most common signs that indicate a detrimental business alliance.

Responsibilities are unbalanced

Labor and supervision should always be equally divided based on each partner's strengths and weaknesses. If you're a particularly creative individual, but you lack in marketing knowledge, for instance, a good partner is one who will bear the brunt of marketing management while allowing you to exercise a greater role in R&D.

Aside from capital and startup funding, dividing labor is the primary reason why many companies opt for partnership. So, before any contracts are signed, make sure that you divide tasks beforehand to make it clear what each of you should expect.

Communication is difficult

Neither partner should make any decisions of serious consequence without consulting the other. The two of you should be able to frequently communicate in person, or at least through emails, to stay in the loop of the happenings on the other side of the boat. If your partner takes a long time to respond to any inquiries or tends to prioritize their own opinions and decisions over yours, this is a red flag that should not be ignored.

There is a significant gap in experience level

The two previous points are oftentimes a result of one partner having more or less experience than the other. Of course, there is no accurate way to measure one's professional experience, but picking someone substantially older than you, and one who has been in the industry for much longer, may result in them taking your views less seriously.

On the other hand, someone who is less experienced may lack the confidence to take any initiatives, which will have you carrying the burden of all business obligations on your own shoulders.

Either of you is unable to compromise

A good business partner is one who could sacrifice an idea that they're emotionally attached to, in the event the second partner disagrees with its efficacy. Misunderstandings between partners are common and cannot be avoided; however, both of you should know how to compromise when you reach a fork in the road.

In that case, partners should put their own interests aside and consider what would be best for the company. Evaluate the decisions in question by pragmatically establishing the pros and cons of each. That way, one or both of you can compromise on your idea for the benefit of the company.

How Do I Find the Right Partner?

You may be surprised to know that the perfect partner for you and your business does not have to understand the intricacies of running a business impeccably. Instead, a partner is someone who can take realistic approaches to help contribute to company growth in one or more areas. Before you decide on a person to trust, ask yourself these questions.

Do we share a vision?

One of the reasons why it's smart to avoid drastically more experienced partners is because they will likely have different goals and an overall philosophy that contradicts yours. Ask your prospective partner where they see the company in several years, and what demographic they expect to cater to. It's crucial to find a partner who does not plan to change the core of your business.

Do we share the same skills?

If the answer is yes, it's time for you to browse other options. It's natural for you to be inclined to find someone as skilled as you are, but those skills should never be the same. It's a bad idea for partners to manage the same department because this could lead to countless disagreements. Instead, choose someone who could manage the departments you're least interested in running (based on lack of skill).

Is my partner confident?

It's not uncommon to find someone whose expertise in a certain field makes them a perfect fit for your company. However, ideas and long-term plans would be for naught if the person in charge is not confident enough to execute them or lead a team that can. Always choose someone confident of their own abilities, yet who has a realistic view of how far their skills can go.

Are There any Legal Measures I Should take Before Partnering?

The short answer is yes. Even if you choose someone whom you have known for years and know you can trust, there is a staple of legal measures that must be taken care of before you sign that partnership agreement.

Authorization of Managerial Decisions

If you don't have a clear list in your partnership agreement that determines what each of you is authorized to do on behalf of the company, the best-case scenario is that your favorite employee gets fired. The worst-case scenario? *You* get fired.

That's right. There have been numerous cases of partners being fired from their own companies by other shareholders. Even Steve Jobs was once fired from his own company after a disagreement with his CEO! Discuss with your lawyer how to incorporate a strict employee-owned policy in your contract.

Percentage of Ownership

You and your partner should always discuss beforehand how much each of you is willing to invest. More funds are not always better, as this will also alter the percentage of your ownership, which also decreases your income.

If it's a small business, you should never opt for more than one partner, and typically one who will contribute a share of less than half. More profit for you means that you can choose to invest more in the business to help it grow in the future, whereas your partner may not be willing to do the same.

Dissolution

If there's anything specific you're worried that your partner may do or refuse to do in the future, all of it should be included in the dissolution section of your contract. This means that your partnership can be *dissolved* or terminated in the event your partner overrides predetermined policies. This could include retirement, sharing confidential information, a change in profit sharing ratio, or simply the expiration of the agreement signed.

How Can a Partnership Go Wrong?

There are many more dangerous risks to consider if you choose to get a business partner, and they are not as simple as miscommunication and having to compromise. In fact, the following reasons are precisely why many startup founders decide against partnership altogether, no matter how much they may need the funds.

Limited Control

The Issue

You're not hiring a manager that you can let go if things don't go your way. An employed shareholder has full control over the division they run, which means that your hands will be tied if you disagree with the way they run their department. Partners *own* the company, too, and they *can* legally take risky decisions on the company's behalf without your knowledge. Of course, you could always add a policy in your agreement that would prevent such blatant behavior, but it's not as simple as that.

Or rather, sometimes, it IS much simpler than that, in that you have no legal way to prevent it. If you don't like how your partner treats employees, for instance, this is not something that could be prevented with a policy in a contract. And while partners may not be able to make big, impactful decisions without your approval, they still have full control over their designated department, which can go downhill if their strategies are faulty.

How to Prevent It

If you think you have the skills to run the company on your own but lack the funds, always opt for a silent partner, who has no say in operational matters and can only contribute to the company via capital. In return, they get their agreed share of the profit.

Loss of a Relationship

The Issue

While your handy business book may not include this risk in the partnership section, you need to understand that you're legally binding yourself to work hand-in-hand with a person for as long as your contract will last – which is, in some cases, forever. If you decide to make your spouse a partner, for instance, this will make the work environment less appealing to you if you ever part ways. Because unlike marriage, you cannot divorce your way out of a business partnership (dissolution notwithstanding).

That said, partnerships may also *lead* to breaking bonds between people. If you choose a friend or family as your partner, the common disagreements that both of you will have to deal with will inevitably impact how you view one another, and in many cases, it can be a cause of losing friends and disliking family members.

How to Prevent It

Avoid making old friends, spouses, or family your business partners, unless it's absolutely necessary. If you have limited options, avoid partnering with someone who can "retaliate" in the business place in the event you grow to be on bad terms in your personal life. For instance, a former spouse is more likely to wreak havoc on your work environment's peace in passive-aggressive ways than a parent or a sibling.

Legal Liability

The Issue

Picture this: it's been a few good years, and your company is seemingly doing great. You check your mail as you have your morning coffee, and you find an envelope with the civil court stamp. You read the letter and spit out your coffee as you read that you have been sued.

Your business partner can cause you to end up in court if they make a corporate decision that violates the law. Lawsuits can be extremely expensive, to the point that they can bankrupt a company. Just because *you* have no say in or knowledge of a small decision doesn't mean you won't be deemed accountable if it violates the law.

How to Prevent It

Partners must make sure that they both understand applicable laws, which in turn can be a burden. You'll feel the need to consistently monitor divisions for which you got a partner to alleviate the need for monitoring. It's pretty counterproductive and can add to the stress of having to run the company, but it is necessary to make sure your company is not executing anything illegal.

Reputation Risks

The Issue

Having your reputation on the line is one of the many risks that your lawyer can't help you with when signing the agreement. How your partner behaves within the company and in their personal life can and will impact your reputation.

How could their personal life affect the reputation of your company? Mostly through social media. It's not uncommon to hear of "cancel culture" putting a company out of business when a founder or partner expresses a bigoted opinion or says something that appalls the public. This is more common with bigger corporations, but you should never underestimate the power of word-of-mouth, even if you have a small business.

How to Prevent It

While it's advised to partner with someone in whom you're not too emotionally invested, your partner shouldn't be a complete stranger, either. Make sure you're aware of this person's views, how they act in stressful situations, and how far you could trust them with your business.

Are There any Other Disadvantages?

Aside from hefty risks, there may be some unpleasant disadvantages of partnership, even when matters go as planned.

Loss of Your Autonomy

So, you've invested every penny you own in a business and worked long and hard so you could make it to the top of the corporate ladder. Having a partner can make operational and financial matters easier, but it also means that you're not fully in charge of the company you worked so hard to start.

Obligatory Business Consent

A general partnership will prevent you from making any monumental operational decisions without the consent of your partner. This may become stressful for many founders, as they always, at heart, see the company as their own, regardless of partners.

Potential Failure in Case of Dissolution

Dissolution doesn't always happen when a partner is shady or dishonest. Sometimes they're obligatory in cases of death or withdrawal. If dissolution occurs when you least expect it, this can make your company financially or operationally unstable.

Why Should I Get a Partnership?

All the previous sub-sections may have covered reasons why you wouldn't want to invest in a partnership, but there are also many benefits if you choose the right partner.

Higher Capital

While the company's income is divided, your partner may have their own network of connections that could help make your company thrive and attract more customers. Having a partner also makes it easier for you to borrow capital to start your business, as this can make your lender evaluate a higher potential profit.

Work/Life Balance

It's not just the extra cash that makes partnerships worthwhile. It's the extra free time you get on your hands when you have someone that has your back. Partners also make it easier to take long vacations, as they can take over when you can't, and you get to return the favor. This will make sure that your company is in good hands when you're away for leisure or emergencies.

Wide Range of Expertise

You could be great at coming up with ideas, but not very good at marketing them. Or perhaps, you want to take over the finances of your company for security reasons, but you don't have the skill for it. Finding a partner who can fill in where you're lacking will multiply your company's chances of success.

Finding a business partner for your company is tricky and cannot guarantee the growth of your business. While it's an efficient way to divide responsibilities, potential risks may outweigh the benefits to some founders. If you need a partner to help you with funding, consider finding a silent partner.

Chapter Six: The Legal Status of Your Business Now and In the Future

When starting a business, choosing the legal business category you want your company to fall under affects how you make income, hire staff, and implement marketing strategies. In other words, that small decision of choosing what document you and your potential co-founders will sign will impact the future of your business. It's not a decision that should be taken lightly or on a whim, and it's best that you fully understand the nature of each type of business entity before you start your business.

That said, choosing the right business entity for your company doesn't mark the end of your legal responsibilities. A myriad of other steps and precautions need to be taken, such as preparing for taxes, potential liabilities, licensing, and any needed permits.

While this section will never replace a lawyer, it will allow you to predict the legal stages of starting a business and will acquaint you with everything expected of you from the legal authorities as a business owner. This guide will also help prepare you for legal complications that you may encounter in the future and help you to avoid or deal with them accordingly.

Entity Types

This sole decision determines the amount of taxes you pay, the loans you could be granted from investors, and your risk exposure in the event your company is sued. Although in most countries, there are tens of business-entity types to choose from, startups generally have the following six options:

Sole Proprietorship

If you don't have any partners or co-founders, a sole proprietorship is a simple, easy-to start business entity that documents you as the sole operator and owner of your business. What makes this entity easy for beginner entrepreneurs is that no corporate formalities need to be documented. Meaning, you won't be compelled to keep track of meeting minutes or other similar reports to pass an audit. Plus, you get to cut your business losses from your tax return.

However, this may not be in your best interest if the business will require hefty funding or loans, seeing as this will make you legally liable for all responsibilities. If your business is sued in the future, this can result in many of your assets being taken away from you as compensation. It may also be more challenging for you to get a business loan because there's little to no legal difference between you as a person and your business. The good news is, you can eventually convert your sole proprietorship company into an LLC or corporation when your business thrives.

General Partnership (GP)

If your company has more than a single owner, your most viable option will likely be a GP entity. This will allow all partners to manage the business and divide profits and losses accordingly. Just like its sole-proprietorship counterpart, you won't be required to register for it, and paperwork is fairly easy. GP entities are just as easy to start; however, the upside is, you won't have to be liable for funding arrangements and debts on your own.

Unless you sign a partnership agreement, this entity may be at risk of failure if disputes between partners do not reach a resolution. It's just as challenging as its sole-partner counterpart to get loans from investors, seeing as your entity is not registered. For early businesses with lower funding, this may be the ideal option, as partners can share liabilities until they can convert their business into another entity type.

Limited Partnership (LP)

While this business entity is not as easy to start, being registered makes it safer and gives your company more options when it comes to funding and finding investors. Paperwork must be filed with the state, and you must document yourself as an active partner, or a general partner, and others as limited partners, also known as silent partners.

Silent partners have no control over how you operate your company but invest in your business in return for an agreed-upon share of the profit determined by their ownership percentage. This business option makes it easier to raise money, as your investors can identify as limited partners and will not be personally liable for any legal issues that your company may face. That said, this entity is far more expensive to start, primarily because it requires a state filing.

It's possible for general partners to avoid personal liability from their peers' actions through a limited-liability partnership (LLP); however, most countries and states only grant this entity to law and accounting firms and doctor's offices.

C-Corporation

C-corps are possibly the most appealing entities to startups and will open doors to various sources of funding for your company, but they're also one of the most challenging and expensive entities to start. C-corps are independent and separate from a company's owner and are also shareholders in the business. So, you have a board of officers and directors running the company (the owners), and investors who fund the project. What makes it appealing is that the owners are not legally liable for any debts or litigation-related liabilities.

This type of entity is also eligible for more tax deductions than any other entity, as the owners pay lower taxes as self-employers.

That said, filing fees are more expensive, and while the company is initially eligible for tax cuts, it also regularly faces double taxation – shareholders tax and corporate tax. Also, shareholders are unable to deduct any business losses on tax returns.

S-Corporation

S-corps are similar to C-corps but have the added benefit of being a pass-through entity, meaning tax returns and deductions are more practical. Through this entity, shareholders are not legally liable for debts, while the corporation's losses are made up for through tax returns. An S-corp does not face double taxation or corporate taxation.

However, for obvious reasons, they're very expensive to start and pose more limits on investing options when it comes to issuing stock.

Limited Liability Company (LLP)

To put it in colloquial terms, LLPs give you the best of both worlds when it comes to liabilities and profit. But as previously mentioned, only a few services are eligible for this entity type, and even then, they may run into more difficulties when it comes to gathering the funds needed to register the company.

LLP companies have fewer paperwork requirements; they essentially operate like sole proprietorships and partnerships, but with added benefits. You have the choice to have the IRS deem you a pass-through entity or a corporation, based on how you want to be taxed. On top of that, corporate formalities are not as strict as those required to run S-corps or C-corps.

When you decide on a business structure, you need to bear in mind that there are other legal requirements that need to be taken care of to ensure that your business will operate smoothly with all the right permits, licensing, and tax preparation methods. Here's what you may need to know.

What Permits and Licenses Do I Need?

This stage of getting your startup on its feet is one of those phases that will have you rushing from one office to the other to get the needed documents. And although there's no way to avoid making this stage tedious, it helps to know the requirements are based on what your business does. Not all these permits or licenses will be required; it all depends on the work environment of your business, and what your product or service involves in the production and management processes.

General Business License

This license essentially registers your business for taxation. Businesses in general are required to have a general business license issued by the city or state. You should expect an inspection of your workplace for an evaluation of public safety and social impact.

This license will also be helpful if your business requires buying wholesale goods, as it will negate additional sales tax.

Fire Department Permit

If your company uses flammable materials, you're going to need a permit from your fire department. This is one of those permits that you must get before opening your business to the public. In some areas, you may not be required to have a permit, but will have periodic inspects that evaluate the safety of your work environment. If you don't meet the safety regulations, a citation will be issued. Any crowded, closed spaces such as daycares or restaurants are subject to these inspections.

Environmental Permit

Although this doesn't apply to all cities, many now have environmental protection offices that work to limit air and water pollution. If your industry burns any materials or disposes any liquids into sewers, a permit is likely needed. If you don't know if you have any environment offices in your city, quick research or a phone call to your lawyer may be of help.

Sign Permit

It usually never crosses an entrepreneur's mind when they place a sign right outside their new working space that they might be doing something against the law. Some cities have regulations when it comes to sign size and location; check your city's regulations, and have your landlord sign their approval before you hang that sign on your office door.

Zoning Permit

A zoning permit determines where your business can and cannot operate, and this also includes home business owners. Depending on your service or product, you may be subject to operating only in certain areas. However, you can counter this by applying for a variance or what's also known as a conditional-use permit to operate in the area which is not zoned for your business.

Professional License

Although the requirements vary according to the city or state in which you wish to operate, professional licenses may be required. This applies to special services ranging from hairdressing to childcare. Professions like accounting will also be required to acquire special licenses.

Construction Permit

If, for any reason, you are rebuilding or altering the construction of your workplace, you will have to obtain a construction permit before you make any alterations.

Federal License

Your business may need a license from a federal agency if it involves activities like manufacturing or selling alcohol or firearms. You'll also need this license for activities related to wildlife, especially those that import or export animals.

Special State License

If you own a restaurant or any other establishment that deals with or serves alcohol to the public, your business will need a special license before it can operate, in order for the state to make sure that your service runs according to specific state standards and regulations. Failing to obtain this license and proceeding with your business may risk shutting it down.

Sales Tax Permit

If your company operates by selling goods, in person or online, your city or state will have to collect sales tax. In that case, a business permit will also be required, which is also known as a seller's permit. It's not as simple as it may seem, as there's a fine line between a service and a product, and oftentimes a service-provider may be required to pay sales tax as well.

What taxes will I have to pay?

Taxes are, unfortunately, not as simple as calculating a percentage of your profit, because there's a convoluted set of different federal, state, and local policies used to assess them. With that said, here are some of the challenges you may face when it comes to tax preparation.

Payroll and Taxes

Each shareholder in a company will be subject to personal taxes on the income they receive, which means that the business in question will have to file federal and state withholding taxes. It gets a little more complicated when you deduct taxes from your employees' paychecks. There are payroll services that make those calculations on your behalf, but startups may find they're paying more for the services than they are in taxes.

If you have employees other than company partners, you must pay worker's compensation and/or insurance, but only if you have more than three full-time employees.

License Fees

Other fees may include an annual sum that you pay if your business is registered with the State Corporation Commission. Any license you have registered for may be subject to an annual fee, so make sure you check your state's regulations to make sure your licenses stay in effect.

Business Structure

The primary factor that decides the taxes you're liable for is the business entity you have chosen for your company. Therefore, it's advisable to opt for limited liability or S-corp structures, as they will protect you from lawsuits and will provide you with plenty of tax advantages and returns. But since it all depends on the kind of service or product your company has to offer, it's best to consult an attorney for in-depth details.

Are There Other Legal Liabilities I Should be Aware Of?

A startup will have to be able to navigate a path of liability roadblocks before they're able to fully operate, which is why it's best to make a checklist of everything you may need to take care of before you launch your startup. These are additional legalities you will likely encounter.

Intellectual property protections

You're going to want to initiate copyrights and trademarks to protect your product from being copied. If you don't get these protections, you might have to face some very costly legal battles with your rivals. These kinds of protections also enhance the commercial value of your company and make it more appealing for both investors and customers. Suppliers, partners, and investors usually like to perform intellectual property checks before they make any agreements with you.

Non-disclosure agreements

These agreements constitute confidential information that may not be disclosed to other parties without the consent of all partners involved in a business. These also determine who owns said information, how long the information should be kept confidential, and how it should be handled. Non-disclosure agreements are issued to contractors, employees, and other third parties to ensure that your confidential business data stays confidential.

Employee contracts

Even startups at their earliest stages will need some employees, even if they're only involved part-time. You're going to have to legally bind them to a contract to protect their rights as well as yours. Many founders hire attorneys to take care of such documentation processes for them. A legal counselor is advised when signing contracts with executives, as some detrimental risks may be incurred if the contract is not drafted properly.

Privacy policies

A startup founder is responsible for managing privacy-policy protections. You will need to make matters transparent when it comes to data usage so that consumers know what they're dealing with and can learn to trust your service or the product you have to offer. These protections don't just make your business more appealing to the public, they also help bulletproof confidential user data from being breached.

Because these steps and precautious may differ depending on where you live, it's important to do some research on your industry and country or state. This guide should cover the legal liabilities you might be subject to, but they cannot replace a legal advisor or an attorney.

Chapter Seven: Your Business Is Born; Naming, Registering, And Insuring Your Business

This section will discuss the naming and registering of your company with the various government entities involved. It will also address how to protect your business by examining the various types of insurance available.

Choosing the company name is as fun as any creative endeavor can be. A lot will enter in to choosing the name.; it isn't just a matter of finding something that resonates with your brand identity, which is obviously still important. Your choice for a business name should take into consideration the fact that it must be unique and not currently in use by another entity.

Naming Your Business

Step 1: Check If the Chosen Name Is Available — Your Entity Name

Your entity name protects you at a state level. For example, if you named your company XYZ, there could exist another company with the exact same name in another state. So, if you have a name in mind, the first step would be to check if it is taken. There are a number of websites that will offer a free check, as well as government-operated websites that will do this specific to the state in which you will register your company.

The entity name is how your company will be legally identified by your state. Different states will have different rules, regulations, and procedures on how to register the name. Some states will even dictate that the company name must reflect the kind of business in which your company will engage. It is highly recommended to check state websites regarding their regulations.

Step 2: Do You Want or Need a Trademark?

The name you chose in step 1 does not protect your company's name outside your state. This means if you want to heavily brand your company and ensure no confusion between yourself and other legal entities, it may be wise to register your company name as a trademark. Trademarks protect you at a federal — national— level. Trademarks can be used for both your company and for goods or services. This comes in handy if your chosen name is desired by competitors in the same or similar industry.

As great as this security may be, it can be a double-edged sword. Infringing on someone else's trademark can prove costly if taken to litigation. The United States Patent and Trademark Office provides a database to check to see if your name, or product, or service names are already used. Follow this link: https://www.uspto.gov/trademark

Step 3: Consider a DBA Name

A DBA (Doing Business As) name is sometimes not required by your state laws but can prove to be beneficial for your company. A DBA may be commonly referred to as a fictitious name, trade name, or assumed name. This oftentimes comes handy if your company handles activity in different business sectors or wants to operate under different names but for the same company. To illustrate this, let's examine a company that owns and operates hotels. This company can have a name like XYZ and can own a hotel like a Hilton franchise, for example. The company could have a legal entity name of XYZ and do business as Hilton Franchise Hotel if that was their registered DBA.

This comes in handy for doing business with a more common name than your registered entity name; multiple people or business can operate with the same DBA in one state.

As with trademarks, filing for a DBA comes with a different ruleset from state to state, and you must consult government offices and websites for the state-specific procedures. Moreover, the rules for a DBA may vary depending on the county and municipality, or even depending on the company structure.

Step 4: Choosing a Domain Name

With the importance of having an online presence in today's market, your domain name is just as important to your company's success as your entity name. A domain name is the same as your website address.

Like your entity name, your domain name must be unique. But this extends beyond the state limitations on entity names, as domain names are worldwide. You must register your domain name through a registrar service. Here is a link to a directory of accredited registrar services: https://www.internic.net/regist.html

Please note that this registrar service is different from the domain- hosting services that actually host your website for you. However, most domain-hosting services will also register your domain name for you. Domain hosts will also explain the WHOIS registry, and how you can protect your company's privacy when registering your domain name.

Registering Your Business

With your names picked out and their availability verified, it is time to make it official and register the company with the government. This can be a multistep process that can be examined at two different levels; federal and state.

Federal Registration

Federal registration is not always necessary, depending on your company's legal structure. For example, if you have set up an S Corp, you will need to file form 2553 with the IRS (Internal Revenue Service).

Most businesses will not actually need to register federally to become a legal entity. But at the bare minimum, your business will apply for a federal tax ID number. This ID number is often referred to as an EIN (Employer Identification Number). An EIN is similar to a TIN (Taxpayer Identification Number) or SSN (Social Security Number) but is for a legal entity as opposed to an individual.

To apply for an EIN, follow the steps below:

- Visit: https://sa.www4.irs.gov/modiein/individual/index.jsp

- Click on Start Application

- Choose the type of company you have and click continue

- Read the information given then click on continue

The process will vary slightly depending on the selections you have made thus far, but as you navigate the website, the information will be provided and explained. Required forms will be available as links to PDF files. At the conclusion of the online procedure, your application for an EIN will be submitted. Remember to fill out the requested information accurately and factually. Oftentimes the website will check some of the information provided, such as your name and SSN, against existing IRS records. Errors here will slow down the completion of this process or may result in the rejection of the application.

More information on how to obtain an EIN can be found on the U.S. Small Business Administration website at the following link:

https://www.sba.gov/business-guide/launch-your-business/get-federal-state-tax-id-numbers.

State Registration

Most likely, you will need to register your company with your state. The scenarios where you are exempt from this are very limited; for example, if you operate under your personal name and have no form of liability protection. In the case of setting up your company as an LLC, corporation, partnership, or nonprofit corporation, you need to register with any state in which you conduct business activity. The extent at which you conduct business in a state resulting in the need for registration involves:

- Your business having a physical presence in the state

- Having frequent in-person meetings with clients or businesses in the state

- Your company's revenue is primarily or heavily contributed to by business in the state

- Any of your employees work in the state

How you register with the state will vary depending on the state. Depending on your state, you may be able to register online, but many states require you to file paper documents, either in person or through the mail. Most states will require you to register with the Secretary of State's office, a Business Bureau, or a Business Agency.

Getting a Registered Agent

If your company is an LLC, corporation, partnership, or nonprofit corporation, you need a registered agent. A registered agent receives official papers and legal documents on behalf of your company. You can list yourself for the role or discuss having your CPA (Certified Personal Accountant) or legal counsel being listed in your place.

State Filing Documents and Fees

Now that you have the information for filing, you need to actually do it. In other words, let's put all the information down on the forms and give them to the government to formally establish your company. As with most government procedures, this will cost money. While the cost for filing varies from state to state, it will generally cost under $300.

The forms you will fill out will ask for your business name and its location, ownership, management structure, or directors, the number and value of shares, and the registered agent information.

The documents you need will differ depending on your company structure.

LLCs will require Articles of Organization and an Operating Agreement, which are, respectively, a document describing the basics of your LLC and a document that describes your company's operations. The operating agreement defines the financial structure and members' roles, duties, powers, and responsibilities. Even if not required by the state, it is strongly recommended you create an agreement for your LLC. Some standardized LLC operating agreements are available for purchase, but you should consider having a qualified attorney draft a personalized agreement for your company.

LPs (Limited Partnerships) and LLPs (Limited Liability Partnerships) will require a certificate of limited partnership and certificate of limited liability partnership, respectively, which are simple documents that describe the basic partnership information to the state. You will also need a limited partnership agreement or limited liability partnership agreement, respectively. This is similar to the LLC operating agreement but created for a partnership as opposed to an LLC. Again, it is recommended you have a qualified attorney create this document.

Corporations will need articles of incorporation and bylaws or resolutions. Articles of incorporation are a comprehensive legal document that lays out the basic outline of your business. The most common information found on the articles of incorporation is the company name, business purpose or scope, number of shares offered, value of said shares, directors, and officers. The corporation bylaws are similar to the operating agreement an LLC would have but structured for a corporation's governance.

To access the required forms or websites, go to your states' Secretary of State website. The following link to the US Small Business Administration will ask you to select the state in which you are setting up your company, and then provide you with links to the relevant website. https://www.sba.gov/business-guide/launch-your-business/register-your-business.

Don't worry if this a lot to digest; it's a lot of business lingo for new business owners, but it's all relatively simple in practice, and you are just filling out forms to establish your company. Your CPA or lawyer can carry out this process for you, and a number of online services, like legalzoom.com, will collect the information online and file the forms for you (for a fee, of course). If you want to do it all solo and are unsure about small details when filling out the form, the staff at the government office should, to an extent, be able to clarify certain points.

Finally, depending on your state, you may be required to file additional documents with your state tax board or franchise tax board. You generally have 30 to 90 days to file these subsequent forms, if they're required.

Insuring Your Company

Currently, it is wise to insure most aspects of life and all aspects of business. Liability litigation is serious and can financially cripple a growing company.

There is a plethora of different types of insurance available for all the different kinds of businesses and their respective company structures. Below you will find some insight into some of the types of insurance available for your business. Please note that this is not an exhaustive list, but further below will be instructions on how to find almost any type of coverage.

Property Insurance

This type of insurance is like home insurance; it covers your business' building and its contents against theft, fire, and, depending on your policy, natural disaster.

Vehicle Insurance

If your business will own and/or operate vehicles, vehicle insurance will help cover you for damages due to accidents or theft. It may cover injuries and offer protection against lawsuits filed against you by other drivers.

Public Liability Insurance

This covers you for harm or damages caused by your business to other people's property or person.

Professional Liability Insurance

This is popular with people offering consulting services such as lawyers, medical doctors, engineers, etc. This insurance covers damages sustained by a client by dint of your professional opinion/advice.

Business Continuation Insurance

If for reasons you can't foresee, your business slows down or shuts down, this type of insurance can compensate you while you get it back up and running.

Key Person Insurance

If you're a small business that has employees essential to its operation, and they stop working due to unforeseen circumstances, this insurance can help cover recruitment costs to replace them.

Shareholder Protection Insurance

Simply put, if a shareholder of your company passes away, this insurance will enable you to buy their now-available shares. This money can often be a good bereavement condolence for the family of the deceased and reduce possible complications from the stock holdings in the deceased's estate becoming a legal issue.

There are countless other types of insurance to consider, like employee liability insurance, workers' compensation insurance, business-specific types of insurance, etc. Knowing which policies your business should purchase is best decided by consulting your lawyer and/or an insurance broker. Insurance brokers will naturally want to sell you as many policies as they can, but they are very good at listing all the types of coverage your business may need.

How Do You Find Business Insurance?

- Research insurance providers; not all of them offer all the various policies.

- Once you find reputable companies set up meetings with brokers from serval firms (at least three different firms).

- Meet with the brokers to see what types of policies they can offer you and shop for the best rates.

Don't take insurance quotes at face value. Insurance policies will have different monthly premiums based on the cap on coverage, the deductible, and other factors. Ask your broker to break these down.

When shopping for insurance, you want to get a watertight (or airtight) policy. Oftentimes insurance companies will try their best to avoid paying a claim, because that's a loss on their balance sheets.

Here are some questions to ask the broker to help you craft a watertight policy:

- What exact type of damages does my policy cover?

- What scenarios would not be covered under my policy?

- Is there a way to be covered for any of these scenarios?

- How long does it generally take for a payout on my policy?

- In the event of a lawsuit, will the policy allow me to hire my own attorney, or must I use one recommended by the insurance firm?

It would be near impossible to exhaustively list the questions needed to be asked; multiple consultations with multiple brokers will aid you in understanding which issues are key and help you find and craft the most cost-efficient policy with the optimal coverage for your business' needs.

By now, you should have a better understanding of how to name, register, and protect your new business. Don't underestimate the importance of any of these steps as they can all be critical to the growth and success of your company. Maintain records and keep copies of all documents pertaining to your company registration and insurance policies. It is also wise to keep digital copies of key documents.

Chapter Eight: Hiring Team Members

Another important aspect of starting your own company is hiring your staff; this is a crucial part of building your company's front men. The first employees you hire are the most important ones; figuring out who they should be isn't exactly easy. But with the right mindset and plan, you'll be able to find the perfect candidates for the job.

Conducting Your First Skill Gap Analysis

Many new startups don't start off well if they skip this step; conducting your first one might be a little confusing if you haven't done it before, but it's essential to help your company get on its feet and moving forward.

The Overview of Your Company

Get a bird's eye view of every position and department that in your business by linking your business goals and company vision to a hierarchy chart. As the employer, use you can see what every position needs, skills-wise, to fill in the gaps with new employees.

Strategic Planning

You need to understand that you're going to go through a series of phases; the business world is always changing and evolving, so you must be ready for it. You need to be able to ascertain with certainty who you should hire and how you should train them to achieve your goals.

A thorough plan can help you with your analysis on two levels: on the individual level and on team level. If you had a workforce now, you'd get them together and talk about what the organization is missing. But since you're just starting up, you're going to jump ahead and find applicants that can fill in those gaps you have with the skills you're looking for. This will serve as groundwork and experience when the time comes to have that chat with your existing workforce.

Identifying Important Skills

Think of not only the skills necessary for the particular job slot, but skills your company would value and appreciate on an ongoing basis. This will help you immensely in narrowing down your applicants.

Measuring the Skills

You need to have a skills spreadsheet that is designed for every position. You don't need to be too strict with your criteria, since you're just starting up, but later you can be a little picky once you have a considerable presence in the business world.

Acting Upon Your Data

Now that you have talked with all the applicants and conducted your assessments, it's time to start hiring and training people. Your employees don't have to be the personification of perfection; you will all learn together along the way as your business is growing. Start choosing the ones you feel would be a good fit for your company, then train the ones that need a little push to be better.

Testing and Training:

Every job has a set of steps and ways to make it go smoothly, so you should test your possible employees on the specifics of the job to see how they would handle it. If they didn't show much aptitude on the test, but they've shown a lot of potential in a hands-on environment, then consider training them through training modules, practice sessions, and on-the-job training so they can get the experience they lack.

Finding People to Hire

This step can be difficult for most startups; thinking about the responsibility of being in charge of other people's livelihood can be scary. But if you manage to locate people that understand the level of risk involved in a startup, then you have nothing to worry about. Just be frank with every person you interview and share with them your idea and vision so they can get invested in it. Some avenues for finding those future employees:

Personal Referrals and Hiring Platforms

As a startup, you should be searching your personal network of people first, asking if anyone is interested or if they have a set of people that they might recommend. Posting on different platforms and social media can also bring in some applicants, just remember to specify what you want and go easy with your requirements.

Have an Online Presence

One of the things you should be doing is building your brand; this should be done early on because it's how you're going to get more people moving. People invest in something that has meaning and a good purpose, and you can show all that online to reach the maximum amount of people. You need exposure, so getting it on different platforms and social media is the way to go. People will be interested in this and want to be part of it; you just need to show them value and unique project ideas.

Don't Limit Yourself with Location Barriers

Even though it's easier to search locally, it's not always the right thing to do. You might need to break down geographical barriers and connect with people around the world. Some positions might be best filled by remote employees; some marketing angles or suppliers might call for an interpreter on the payroll.

The Educational System

Forming strong relationships with different colleges and universities can bring in top-tier candidates for you; think of it as having the professors or teachers to do the recruiting for you. Young graduates are motivated, hungry for knowledge, and smart with their bright new ideas. They would get a chance to be part of something interesting and could be one of the founding employees who are the cornerstone of your business.

The Interview Process

Remember to follow these specific ideals when you're interviewing people:

Assessing and Evaluating

Each person you interview needs to understand that this is the beginning of a journey; be honest with them about the possible risks, but also be open about the company's idea and your vision as an owner/employer. You need to see if they are eager to build this idea with you, show great potential and willingness to work on hard problems; you need people that like a challenge, that love the idea of being part of something new that could change the business world for the best.

Finding Potential

You will find it easier with time and practice to see the potential in people just from their first interview. Understanding their skills and passions and how a specific position can unleash their full potential can mean a lot for your business. You don't have to be focused on their track record, past successes, diplomas and degrees; you should see it in their eyes, in how they talk if they're truly interested and willing to go above and beyond for your company.

Key Traits to Consider

You should consider traits like multi-tasking, quick decision-making, being team players, being independent and strategic thinkers, and being a cultural fit. If you find people that embody these traits, then that can mean a lot to your business; you have strong, bold people who are not afraid, but if they are, then they won't keep it to themselves. You need people who have a voice and an ability to stand up and tell you something and how they feel the business would benefit from it. If they fully understand your vision and core values, any new idea that can further the process should be more than welcome.

You need to realize that finding these founding employees is extremely important, and you should ask them the right questions when you're conducting the interview. Here are some examples of what you should be asking your candidates:

Can You Describe Yourself?

This is important for you because it gives you a little more insight into the person you're talking to, understanding what makes them tick and what's important to them. You will know the person a little better based on their response to this question. This will help you when you narrow down your list of candidates, figuring out who was genuine and who is being cheesy or overdoing it.

In your opinion, what do you think your strengths and weaknesses are?

When you ask them about their strengths, you are getting an idea of their attributes that qualify them for the job. As for their weaknesses, that's a way to see if they can be honest and describe something in themselves that they know needs improvement.

Tell us about your last project - what went well and what didn't?

Leaving this question open-ended so they can choose what to talk about is great for seeing your potential employees using their own words to describe past successes or failures. You will get some insight into how they deal with hardships or sudden circumstances, listening to them talk about what they learned and what they should have done to avoid the problem.

What's the best advice you've received?

It's important to understand how well a person takes in input and criticism, that's why asking this question will let you know if they got some recently and how they handled it. Did they show understanding and take it under advisement? Or did they feel that they "are better than this", and show egocentric behavior?

Why do you believe you're a good fit for the company?

This question can give you an idea of why this candidate deserves the job by linking the answer to your company's goals and working environment. You will be able to gauge if there exists a mutual starting point for a good and beneficial professional relationship between both of you.

What can you do that can benefit us?

Their answer to this question, obviously, alerts you to specific ways they can contribute to your idea and cause.

What are your new ideas that you could apply to this position?

It's important to understand the job description and what one is supposed to do, but it's equally important to have the ability to think on one's feet. Creative ideas and thoughtful strategies can highly benefit a startup company like yours; their answer shows that they are willing to come up with solutions if the situation demands it.

What are you going to do if you don't get the job?

This might discourage your candidate, but it has a hidden motive; the question shows you who thought of alternatives and other steps that can help them reach their goal. This is a prime indicator as to how well they think out the future, possible risks, and contingency plans. This is a highly desirable mindset to have in your company.

Can you tell us something about... (anything unrelated)

You don't need to ask them this if you don't want to, but think about the stages in your company when it's just starting out. There might be times where people will do things that aren't exactly part of their job description, thinking out of the box and helping out just to keep things running smoothly. This is why the sudden change to an irrelevant question can give you an idea of how your applicants respond to changes that they didn't see coming. That's what makes a startup exciting, because the atmosphere will always be that way.

The Legalities

Now that you're going to hire people, it's time to do the paperwork and go through everything by the books that match your government's registration requirements, insurances, payroll, and tax forms. Here's a step-by-step list on how to do this right:

Employer Identification Number

You need to obtain this to use on the tax returns along with other documents to be submitted to the IRS or other tax administrations.

Proper Registration

You need to submit all the needed payments and documents to the labor department in your area; you must state unemployment compensation taxes. These taxes go to a relief fund that helps people who lose their jobs.

Workplace Safety Measures

You must have proper documentation that states you complied with the requirements of your locale's safety procedures and hazard-reduction terms as well as with the Occupational Safety and Health Act. You should keep safety records that have details regarding any workplace accidents or possible irregularities that can be submitted to your government's safety administrators.

Compensation Insurances

This might not be required of you since you're just a small company starting out, but that varies from one area to another. You need to have workers'-compensation coverage to protect your employees if they suffer on-the-job injuries. As a starting company, you can't afford any unnecessary lawsuits, so playing it safe is the way to go.

Employee Benefits

This purely depends on how much capital you have as an owner. Some startups might not have any benefits at first, like social events or health insurance, in which case it's still good to think about what you will need to do later in the way of benefits programs.

Report to the New Hire Reporting Agency

Each area or state has a reporting agency that helps the government track each new employee, do background checks, and see if they have past felonies or owe child support that they haven't paid yet.

Contracts

This is important because it will state everything that is required of you as an employer as well as what is required of the employees working for you. This contract would specify the job descriptions, probation periods, rules of the workplace, the net and gross salaries that they would be getting and how taxes will be processed by you as their employer.

Personal Records

It's important to have files such as tax forms, medical records, performance evaluations, and immigration status (if it applies) for every employee under your payroll.

Payroll

You need a proper system to withhold taxes, meaning that you withhold a portion of each employee's income for forwarding to the IRS or tax administrations. There should be forms like W-4 that each employee signs after filling out any allowances they're claiming for taxes; this helps you withhold the right amount from their monthly paychecks. Remember to prepare the W-2 forms that detail the annual filings to be submitted at the end of each year. Some companies have a banking system where the taxes go into their accounts on a monthly basis, or they have to go to the finance department and get the cash themselves. This depends on what kind of plan is perfect for you at the specific time; consider a software that can assist you in this to keep things from getting out of hand at some point.

Let's be frank, you are just starting up and entering an ocean full of big fish who think you're just a minnow. So, this isn't going to be easy for you at the beginning, but it's your job to attract the right people by showing them the true vision you have and the value you can provide. If you manage to get people that share your core values and understand your vision, then your business will boom with success.

Chapter Nine: Marketing & Promoting

Having people know who you are and what you stand for is key to your company's success; it will take time to get the exposure you need, but spreading the awareness about your brand is vital to getting more customers and clients to invest in your products and services. You need to think about your marketing strategy and how you can utilize the digital world to assist you, allowing you to reach more people faster.

Working on Your Brand

Branding is one of the major reasons why a company could succeed or fail; this is why you need to connect with your target audience and have them interested in your products and services. This will eventually lead to more purchases and subscriptions, so you need to differentiate your company with branding in the correct way.

The Target Market

One of the first steps to a successful branding process is figuring out who you're trying to reach. Ask yourself, who would be the audience with whom you'd want to share your vision? You need to understand that you can't succeed without your customers, so you must find the ideal ones that can be a part of your company's identity. There should be a relationship with your customers and clients wherein they can constantly give you feedback and opinions on how they perceived your products and services. You need people to have good experiences that they are quick to share with others, garnering you more customers in the process.

Investing in a Graphic Designer

This might be difficult for some startups, but it can be worth the investment. Try not to complicate things, though; it doesn't have to be super-perfect and flashy. Talk to your designer and explain your vision, story, and goals. He/she will be able to create multiple graphics that relate to all of it, allowing you to pick and choose those you think would be best. Friends or family that have a graphics-designing background might be much cheaper and easier for you but remember not to spare too many expenses because that can lead to difficulties in the future, possibly making you change everything and start from scratch again.

The Name and Image

Your next step is to come up with a decent visual language with a tagline that sticks, attracting people and making them turn heads to your logo, name, and slogan. You need something that looks appealing and makes a nice first impression. Try to be consistent, brief, and clear to every one of your targets; think about creating something resonates within the people, something that isn't too bold, macho, corny, vague, or forgettable. Also, people don't connect with generic names that much these days, so you should think about creating something with a made-up word that can possibly be the language of your company, one that matches a catchy slogan and keeps it memorable.

Create Great Experiences

This might be hard at first because your company is still a newcomer in the business world, but later this will be one of the reasons why people like you and want to continue investing in you. You should make something for them that they would remember, something that can make you stand out from your competitors. You might consider being a cause-driven company that people relate to because you are showing that you care. Or you could do something that defies expectations, doing something that might be unorthodox and fresh. But be careful not to make people upset, that might backfire right back at you, especially when you're starting out.

Getting Involved in the Local Community

This might not be possible for you at the beginning, but if you do this right, you could be looking at a whole new level of awareness. People won't forget about you if you do something that benefits the community they live in; it helps raise your business profile among all your potential customers. To be involved, you could start donating to a local charity group or doing volunteer work to help them out. Or you could sponsor local events, giving the impression that your company is community oriented. You could contribute to a fundraiser for a local hospital or school; there are any number of ways to make the locals like you more and feel comfortable with your brand because they can trust you and your morals.

Your Business Website

It is a pivotal step to create a website for your company, and if you don't have one, then you'd be missing out on a lot of opportunities and possible leads. Let's take a look at why it's so important to have one:

- Credibility and showing people that you are a legit company.

- It helps your business grow by accomplishing various marketing strategies.

- It generates more feedback from customers to be better.

- Gives your clients and possible new leads a chance to contact you or purchase something you offer.

- Brings in healthy traffic through different SEO (Search Engine Optimization) tactics that can increase your exposure and possible deals.

- It increases your presence and visibility online and in general.

- It helps you save money on big marketing campaigns because it's cost-effective.

- Customers have 24/7 access to what they want, whether it's information, support, and news on upcoming products.

- You will see a considerable boost in sales through your online shop features.

- It increases your overall reputation.

- It gives you a chance to make royalty programs and reward schemes.

- You can add testimonials and facts from different clients later along the road to increase opportunities for leads and profits, showing everyone how good you are.

- It helps you level the playing field against bigger multinational corporations when it comes to rankings.

- Ease of access and convenience that makes people's lives much easier, which will more likely lead to more sales and profits.

- You can show people your vision, telling your story easily to people overseas.

- It would be a way for people to subscribe to weekly newsletters or notifications about new products and discounts.

Marketing Your Business

Let's be honest, you need inexpensive ways to get maximum awareness and cover a huge scale of the market with your presence. This is why digital marketing can be your number-one method of reaching people.

You're your own boss now, and an entrepreneur that wants to see results from your hard work; getting those results would be much easier if you utilized the digital world. Here are some ways of utilizing the digital world to get those results:

Social Media

This is one of the strongest and most effective ways to market a business these days; almost every one of your customers and potential new ones have an account on one, two, or several social media channels. Whether it's Twitter, Facebook, and/or Instagram, a social-media portal is considered to be the easiest method to enhance your online presence and help you generate a big percentage of leads. It can be done through a series of posts that are both creative and appealing, so people don't scroll down and ignore it. Create fun and engaging questions, submit videos related to your business and idea, keep things interesting by posting every day to keep people reeled into your page. You can engage with your audience easily and build strong connections; this leads to more loyal customers that follow you and what you post. You should show everyone that you care by answering everyone's questions and concerns; you can establish brand awareness, and more people will know what type of services and products you're offering. You can expand your business in various ways thanks to social media, so use it to market your brand and get more prospects.

Mobile

74% of people in the world use their smartphones to search for something they need. Therefore, you should have your website mobile-friendly; that can radically increase the number of visitors that check your website. Optimizing your platforms and strategies to be compatible with mobile can mean a lot for your business. You can have small ads on popular apps that people use every day; people are bound to see your name and brand as they're using their phones.

Another way of marketing yourself through the mobile world would be something to consider in the future, when your business has solidified its position and you have the funds for it: you could create your own mobile app, something that relates to your business or service that you're offering.

Email

This is a strong method of promoting your business by tailoring emails specifically to each customer; you can do this by knowing what the customer wants and needs, then allowing them to get it. People love personalized emails that are directly based on what they're after at a specific time; if they're searching for something similar to what you have to offer and you hand it to them on a silver platter, the sale is a done deal. Eventually, these people will become your frequent and loyal customers, investing in your services and purchasing your products.

Marketing automation methods are still an important part of promoting your business easily and you won't have to pay outrageous amounts to reach people. You can nurture your customers with follow-ups and new things that would interest them by syncing everyone's profile with your current CRM system. That way, they would be placed into your workflow, and the correct emails would be sent to the right people.

Special Offers

People love good deals; it might mean less money for each product you sell, but the sales volume going through the roof would surely ease the pain. You increase your profits over time that way.

The methods you could apply range from discounts, seasonal offers, and special coupons sent through emails or mobile ads, to offers for people to buy in bulk to get it all at a lower per-item price.

The discounts could be small codes given to them as they purchase something or sent to them through their emails to use later. Your coupons can be physical ones or E-coupons if you want it to be more convenient for them, saving you a little money in the process, too. A seasonal or special occasion is the perfect time for you to implement some discount offers. That's why there are so many great deals offered at Christmas time; the pros know that a huge boost in sales volume easily outweighs a small decrease in sales margins.

The Approach to Your Customers

If you're thinking about what kind of business you're planning to be, have you thought about being a customer-driven company? People love it when they feel they have been heard and supported every time they have a concern, request, or specific feedback. As an entrepreneur that wants to change the world of business, you can start by showing people that you offer more than just some goods or services; you offer the value that people can appreciate and a brand that they can trust. It's just the way of things in the business world; happy customers mean more referrals, increased sales, extra exposure, immense growth, and plenty of profits. This is exactly what your business would need to move forward and boom with success.

Handling Reviews

This is extremely important because you want people to be heard, thanked, and supported, especially when it's a bad review. Do not shun or ignore unpleasant reviews because that would be a sign of not caring about what people think; you are bound to upset some people along the way because, sadly, we cannot appease every single person in the world all the time. So, the way to handle an unpleasant review is to thank them for their feedback, apologizing for any inconvenience or for their bad experience.

Then you should contact these people who wrote the bad reviews and get a better understanding of what happened and how they feel about it; remember to be calm, supportive, and never accuse people or get defensive. Try as hard as you can to either solve the problem or compensate them in any way possible; this will increase your image by showing people that you care. As for the good reviews, you should reply in kind and thank them for their kind words and loyalty. I know this is difficult but try to not sound too robotic with your replies.

Customer Service and Complaints

Do you know why most startups fail so soon? One of the reasons is not having a proper customer service plan that caters to people that need assistance or need to file a complaint. Let's dive into how you should respond to people with complaints or concerns through the famous five P's in customer care:

Professional

You must focus on rectifying the issue or problem, not the customer's tone or behavior; you should be sincere and humble in your responsive. So, you should never lash out or become hostile with the customer. Ask them for more details and listen to every word, then reiterate it in your own words to make sure that this is what they said and to prove that you listened. Remember to always try to see the problem from the customer's point of view.

Prompt

You shouldn't let a negative comment hang in the air for long without being answered; your window of reply should be within 24-to-48 hours, maximum. People need to feel that their problem is acknowledged, even if you don't have a solution to it, just reply to let them know that they've been heard.

Personal

People hate it when they get a robotic or automated response; they want to hear something genuine, friendly, and respectful. People like it when they are heard, validated, and made to feel justified. Try to be normal and approachable and use simple words that are easy to follow and understand, make them feel at ease and believe that you care about resolving this issue for them.

Polite

It's difficult for some people to stay calm and professional when they get negative comments; you might take it personally and get angry but remember that it's not your place to judge. Even if the customer is being unreasonable or unfair with their comments, you should never reply thoughtlessly with haste and anger. Remember to see the issue from their perspective; you should show empathy and compassion because that's how they would calm down. Remember to apologize, even if it's not your fault.

Private

Remember that people want to be validated and heard, but it doesn't always require a public conversation for everyone to see. Respond and acknowledge them for sure but invite them to have a little chat privately either by phone or email. There are some cases where discretion is needed, and you must judge the situation, whether it requires a private or public response. Also, people feel comfortable and talk freely when it's private and not visible to thousands of people watching.

It would be awful if you created an amazing and useful idea, but you can't make anyone notice what you've created, or it's not appealing at all for people to try what you have to offer. That's why promoting and branding is crucial; every startup can face a lot of problems when it comes to marketing and without it, the business might fail drastically, so remember to put in a lot of thought on how you're going to let people see you and remember you. Also, focus on customer care and make them feel heard.

Chapter Ten: Scaling & Growing

Starting the business is the easy part — ok, it's not exactly easy, but things tend to get more complicated as we move forward. Getting past initial challenges in terms of finances, paperwork, and documentation, and hiring the right team is one thing, but growing the business is a whole other ballgame.

It doesn't matter if it's a bakery, law firm, or online store. As a business owner, you want to grow and expand — and in turn, reach more people and make more money. This is the end goal for any business owner, or at least the serious ones. It's not about having an extra income for the sake of it; that business is your baby, and just like an actual one, there comes a time where it needs to grow and flourish.

A lot of business owners try to bite off more than can chew, and they end up hindering the progress of the company instead of taking it forward. Like anything else in life, timing is everything. Whether it's asking the girl you like out or scaling up your business, you need to find just the right moment, and that can be a bit tricky. Fortunately, there are some signs and indicators that it is time --

and now might be the moment when you can start working on growing and expanding the business to take it to the next level.

Signs That it Might be A Time to Scale Your Business

Demand and supply

One of the biggest mistakes some small businesses do is trying to expand without making sure they have it figured out in terms of demand and supply. You might be achieving some impressive numbers right now, but that doesn't mean that will continue to happen in the future. This is why you need to thoroughly consider whether or not you have enough demand – and supply – to support your efforts to grow.

Scaling your business is expensive, and it will cost you a lot of money and effort. The question is, can your current and, more importantly, future projected supply help you get there? If the answer is yes, then this is the first sign that you might be ready to scale your business. But you really need to be certain of the answer to this question, because it quite literally might save you from going bankrupt while trying to expand. Do you have enough customers right now? Do you expect to get more in the future at a consistent rate than ensures you'll have steady cash flow while trying to grow your business? These aren't the kind of questions you could answer overnight. You need to do thorough research and accurate forecasts to predict whether you can not only maintain your current level but also exceed it while trying to expand.

On the other hand, it's not just the demand that you should take into consideration. You might be getting all the demand you need, and then some, but you can't supply. Can your business/small factory/store cover your current and future needs? It would be nonsensical to try and open a new store or in a different city or country when you can barely cover the current requests you get on a regular basis. This brings us to the following point.

Having enough manpower

Scaling your business requires being able to support your efforts with the necessary experienced manpower. Sure, you can hire new people wherever it is you're trying to expand, but they can't exactly get going on their own — they'll need training, and people who know the business processes to teach and guide them. Think of it that way, if you only have two people running your entire operations — each with a very specific and important role that is indispensable — does it really make sense to send one over to the new location and hope the other can handle all business operations on their own? It definitely wouldn't. But if you have enough team members to carry on with the job even if some of their colleagues got preoccupied with something else, then yeah, it might be a good idea to go for some scaling up.

Finances are good

Needless to say, trying to grow your business with insufficient funds is a bad idea that will not end well for you or the business. You must make sure your finances are in order before you try scaling up because, as we mentioned earlier, expansion is costly, and it will require some significant investment on your side. We talked about the importance of projected demand, but you need to consider other factors in the equation if we're talking about expansion.

Even if you can and will get the required supply in the future that can sustain you, will the money coming off those deals be enough? Are you trying to go overseas, and there's a currency change which might even cost you more? What will happen if there is an unforeseen obstacle, and how will you deal with it? In other words, you can't just rely on the fact that you will have enough demand in the future. You need to do the math and make sure that demand can sustain you financially while taking into consideration other factors like currency fluctuations and conversions, emergencies, and unexpected costs. This is why it is advisable that you only go forward if you are 100% certain your finances are good and can, in fact, sustain your growth plan. It helps if you already have an emergency fund that you can tap into in case things go south.

Original goals are exceeded

Any business starting out sets certain goals. They can be anything from reaching certain numbers to covering initial investments. Another indicator that it may be time to scale is reaching and exceeding those previous goals. But they need to be the big ones you set for yourself when you first started out — paying your employees' salaries on time isn't exactly an indicator you should try scaling. If you find that your business is consistently reaching and exceeding any goals it sets for itself, then perhaps scaling is the solution.

You cannot let your company linger in a comfort zone, because it can be extremely difficult to get out of those. You need the challenge because this is how you, the employees, and the company grow and learn. So, once you're there, and goals are met, start setting higher ones pertaining to an expansion plan that will help you scale up and reach new heights, achieving those new targets and then moving on to even greater ones.

Your team is ready

The most valuable asset a company has is its people, and you can't possibly move forward with your plans to expand and grow without making sure your people are ready for such a step. This doesn't just pertain to their performance and numbers, but what they think and need. It's imperative that you conduct meetings with your people, from middle and upper management to regular employees. Ask them what their problems are and what they think about current plans to grow. You need their input, and you can rest assured they will have useful input — after all, it's they who do the job. Their insight can help you alter your plans, if necessary, and come up with new strategies.

People might be resistant to change, and if your team is not on board, then maybe you should rethink your decision to scale up right now. You could hire some fresh blood who would be more susceptible to change and infuse them with old members to help smoothen the transition. The important thing is having the majority of your team on board, because you are going to need them.

One more angle that you need to cover when it comes to your team is making sure your people are up to date with technology. We live in a world driven by technology, and any business relies heavily on it, one way or another. And before you can scale up, you have to make sure that your company is using the proper and most recent technology.

Factors Hindering Attempts to Scale Up and Grow

Being behind on technology

Picking up from our last point, if your company is using obsolete technology, you probably stand no chance of expansion and growth. You can rest assured that your competition is using the latest technologies and solutions, and if you want to keep up and conquer new markets, you must do the same. It can be anything from cloud solutions to AI and internet marketing strategies; just find out what technologies you need to grow your business and start training your people to leverage them before you even consider scaling up. We live in a digital age, and a company that wants to expand needs to be leveraging state-of-the-art technologies to make it happen.

Rushing the process

We talked about the importance of doing studies and crunching the numbers to figure out just how well you'll do in the future in terms of demand, supply, and finances. A lot of businesses, unfortunately, try to skip past those steps and rush into the process of scaling the company and expanding without proper studies and calculations. The problem is, rushing things without careful consideration not only promises poor results for the scaling up, but it also jeopardizes the integrity of what you've built so far.

It happens quite often that companies rush into expanding to new markets and find halfway through the process that they don't have enough funding to do it. So, they start tapping into reserves and company funds, leading to catastrophic results like not being to pay your bills or even the salaries. As a result of poor planning and rash decision making, the company might have to declare bankruptcy. So, impulsively trying to scale up the company can lead to failure on all fronts.

Not doing market research

The bottom line is, you're presenting a service or a product to consumers. And if you don't know what those consumers want, the entire process is doomed to failure. While you may have done proper market research before starting your business, you need to do it again before trying to expand. If you're trying to conquer a new market, you must ask yourself, is there even room for what I'm offering? Do the people there really need my services? If you want to add a new line of products, for example, you can't do so on a whim. You must be 100% certain there is demand for that product, and that people will buy it.

This is why it's important to conduct thorough market research before any steps to expand your business. The last thing you need is trying to invade a saturated market or offering a new product/service that no one really needs or even asked for. Running a business should never be subject to personal opinions and prejudices, but rather thorough research and careful planning.

Poor infrastructure

One of the biggest reasons why businesses fail in their expansion attempts is not having the proper infrastructure and processes in place before embarking on such a step. Any company starting out needs quite some time to figure things out and come up with its own process, from how people log in their time out/in to how they receive and perform their daily assignments. If those processes, both simple and intricate, are not properly in place, your expansion has no hope of success.

From continuous training to productivity tracking and quality assurance, everything needs to be in place, and all the boxes must be ticked before you try to open a new branch or merge with another company. Chaos is the one thing that can plunge the company into failure, and order does the exact opposite.

How to Scale Your Business

Evaluating your options

The first step to trying to scale your business is evaluating your options and carefully planning what the next step is going to be. We talked about the importance of figuring out your finances and employee readiness, but there are several other factors that you need to consider. For starters, how do you want to scale up your business? Expansion needs thorough preparations and planning, but you first need to figure out which in direction you'd like to take your business. Are you looking to increase your sales by introducing a new product or enforcing a new strategy? Do you want to open a new branch somewhere else? Or are you looking to merge your company with another?

It's important that you evaluate your options to find which direction is best for your business in the long run. Then, as mentioned earlier, you should move to evaluate the readiness of your people, your finances, and future projections. Again, the success of your scaling up attempts rests solely on how well you plan for it and evaluate your different options. So, take it slowly and cover all the angles, because the slightest misstep puts your entire company in jeopardy.

Getting the funding

Earlier in this chapter, we talked about the importance of having it figured in terms of supply and demand, as well as having your finances in order. But what if all the other signs are there and everything is good to go, except for funding? In that case, if funding is really the one thing stopping your business from growing and expanding, then you should consider getting it from alternative sources.

Fortunately, we live in a time where entrepreneurship is on the rise, and there are a lot of willing parties that can help your company grow and reach its potential. Take angel investors and accelerators, for instance, who usually supply smaller companies with the necessary funds for such expansion in exchange for equity. You also have small business contests where they compete for a cash prize that could be anything from $10,000 to $100,000, like the FedEx Small Business Grant Contest. Entering those contests, you don't need to give equity to anyone; just present a kickass plan and impress the judges, and the prize would be yours.

You could also go for a loan, though that should be your last resort. But they sometimes really help and can procure you the funding you need to expand and grow your business. The important thing is not letting funding get in the way of your company's growth and expansion if everything else says it's the right time to start.

Network

No matter what approach you plan on taking with your business expansion, networking is a crucial angle in which you'll need to excel. Scaling a company up is about connections and the people you know, and the more you grow your networks and meet new people who could help you, the better your chances will be. True, you need to be good at what you're doing, but expanding a company requires knowing the right people to help you achieve your goals. Go to social events, startup competitions, and summits, and reach out to mentors and experienced individuals. This will help you form a powerful network that will put you in another city — or even country — or inspire you to come up with new ideas to grow your business.

Hiring the right staff

You have two major assets in your quest for expansion: the people and the technology. If one of those two pillars is missing, your chances of scaling your business up are slim to none. We've already talked about technology and how you need to use the latest in order to stay in the game, but without people to use that technology, it will be worthless. You need to rely on your current team, yes, but you will probably need to hire some new people to help you achieve your goals. If you can't find the exact quality you need right now, maybe it is time to consider outsourcing some of your departments. For instance, expansion requires having a dedicated and professional customer service team, which you might have not had in your current structure. It would definitely take a lot of time to interview, hire, and train customer service personnel, so in a case like this, it'd be best to outsource the entire process.

That way, you'll get pre-trained agents who know how to handle customers, and all you would need to do is train them in *your* process and how to handle the specific details of *your* company. You'll most likely be saving money as well because outsourced services tend to be a lot cheaper.

Dream big

While this might be something taken out of one of those self-development books, in truth, dreaming big is one of the most crucial angles to scaling up your business. If your company is currently worth one million dollars, what's to stop it from being worth ten or a hundred million? If you are going to expand, set high goals for yourself, because if you aim big and put in the effort and time, you'll make it. This won't happen overnight, and it will take a lot of blood, sweat, and tears, but with the right mindset and experienced team, you can get there.

Growing your business might be the most challenging aspect of your entire journey, but it is worth it. To see your team grow in front of you and more people getting to know your brand are things that will make all the time and effort you spent on this process worthwhile. The important thing is giving this phase its due planning and putting in the time and effort to ensure it will work out without undue complications.

Conclusion

In the last decade, an entrepreneurial revolution has been on the rise. Although there are more than 400,000 entrepreneurs to date, only fifty percent of new companies survive the rising competition. Possibly, one of the many reasons why entrepreneurship has become so popular is because today's post-industrial business world is almost completely reliant on the internet. And that doesn't just apply to networking. There are now classes dedicated entirely to the study of entrepreneurship, paving the way for new independent business owners to introduce their products and services to the market.

Perhaps our era's consistent economic decline was what inspired this sudden rise of business startups in the last few decades. More individuals are now coming to realize just how much more lucrative it is to leave their nine-to-five jobs behind and work on their own startup, while the appeal of becoming one's own boss undoubtedly remains a factor in this so-called "startup revolution".

This phenomenon may leave many wondering whether this is just another ephemeral fad in the business world that will inevitably die mainly because of the number of failing startups in the market, some of which don't survive more than a few months. But the underlying cause of these failures is certainly not a flaw in the revolution itself but is due to the media's elusive portrayal of how business moguls have come to succeed. Many an aspiring business owner has attempted to start a business from scratch based purely on the kind of business myths that threaten every entrepreneur.

These myths usually revolve around a warped idea of following one's passion, selling ideas to the first investor you come across, and creating a business with limited knowledge of market demands and basic business development know-how. That said, many entrepreneurs start businesses as an escape from corporate life. And while a successful business doesn't have to be completely unique, solely staring a business to jump on a trending bandwagon is one of the reasons behind many business failures.

This book has covered the importance of other aspects than good business ideas, but that's only because they tend to be overlooked. That surely doesn't mean that an individual with no coherent business model and goal, other than a quick way to make money, will see success. On the other hand, entrepreneurial success is not as challenging as many of today's publications may make it seem.

You'll often see some staggering numbers of failing businesses that never got to see the light despite their promising goals and ideas, but that's usually because the founders of such businesses lacked the skills needed for their business. Most business ideas are born out of need – future founders run into a problem with no immediate solution and decide to create one, for themselves as well as the public. The initial enthusiasm that sparks out of that ah-ha moment usually instills a sense of impatience and irrational anxiety. Oftentimes, entrepreneurs want to implement their ideas as quickly as they can before anyone else makes the same discovery, though the chances of that are slim. And the hasty decisions that arise from this impatience is what eats through the potential of what could have been a billion-dollar idea.

On the other hand, many aspiring entrepreneurs are aware of the importance of developing a compelling business model and dedicate years to the process of perfecting a solution to a problem before they begin their search for possible funding sources. While going into the nitty-gritty of a product before launching it is certainly a smart move, future founders should always cash in as soon as they build a basic business model. This is primarily because cashflow issues may take years to be resolved but should ideally be dealt with simultaneously with product development to shorten the time it takes for the company to launch.

Of course, business prototypes should always be offered to the public on a small scale for feedback before launching, which is another reason why a startup may fail. On the other hand, founders don't have to wait until their service or product is completely impeccable before they make it accessible. Many startups offer reasonably ready services and immediately amend anything that customers complain about.

All these issues that entrepreneurs run into may be the cause of failure, but it's certainly not because entrepreneurship is going out of fashion, or because recent graduates have abused the entrepreneurship path. In fact, all these new companies that offer outstanding solutions to the public are increasingly changing the industry for the better. There is no limit to just how many successful startups penetrate the market, but only those who develop the skills needed for their business thrive. This is possibly the only obstacle that may be standing in your way.

While this book has been written essentially to help new entrepreneurs succeed, the best way to avoid failure is by familiarizing yourself with *why* startups fail. It's certainly not because some founders are luckier than others, and it's not a matter of being discovered and running into just the right people that would help you on your road to success. The only individuals you should count on are your partners and yourself. Business success is an equation that can be learned, and that's what this book aims to help teach you.

Reading as many sources as you can on the field of your choice will be your handy tools before you begin developing your idea. If you already have an idea in mind, build a basic prototype and ask for critique from your trusted partners before you begin your search for potential investors.

Finally, always bear in mind that in some rare cases, the current market will not yet be ready for your product. Many founders who have been ahead of their time with their innovative solutions have eventually found success when they chose to launch at just the right time. Sometimes, products are best kept in development until the market need for them arises.

Part 2: Accounting
A Comprehensive Guide for Beginners Who Want to Learn About Basic Accounting Principles, Small Business Taxes, and Bookkeeping Requirements

Introduction

This book discusses the core concepts and basics of accounting, providing you with a balance of theory and practical examples. Accounting is a vast concept with a wide range of uses, and if you run your own small business, knowledge of accounting and bookkeeping will give you the edge. Most accountants have expert-level knowledge, which allows them to provide top-level consulting services. Whether you have an accountant and want to learn more about it, or you're just starting in business and need to learn how to do it yourself, this book has you covered.

We cover the relevant tools, techniques, and methods used by today's accountants. Given that bookkeeping and accounting are primarily digitized now, we have ensured that the information is streamlined to the new technological techniques rather than outdated manual techniques.

From explaining the Chart of Accounts to the more creative ways to set up your accounting systems, we have made sure that you understand the full extent of the automated tasks while keeping the core ideas of accounting and other principles intact. The successful approach to running your business is to have people who perform these tasks but, we remembered business owners who can't afford to hire an accountant or consult one because of the high cost of a consultation.

Think of this guide as a "first-aid" guide to bookkeeping and accounting. Refer to it when you need help on the basic accounting principles, need to brush up on your skills, or even if you want to check up on what your bookkeeper or accountant is doing.

And discussing financial analysis tools and methods, we also cover taxation and its importance to business performance.

This book differs from all the other similar books on the market because we have taken the time to write it in an easy-to-read manner and explain any necessary jargon. So, if you are ready to take your first steps into accounting and bookkeeping, let's dive in.

Chapter 1: What is Accounting (and Can I Do It on My Own)?

Is accounting rocket science?

Will I be able to run my business without an accountant?

These are a few of the main questions you might ask yourself when running a business or considering becoming an accountant yourself. What do you think an accountant is, and what is the main idea or concept behind accounting?

To start, let's use a typical life example to illustrate that we perform accounting in our everyday lives. For instance, we may have a limited budget for the week's groceries, and we have to decide where best to spend the money to get the most value. You have to decide if you need that expensive brand or a lower brand will do just as well. You also have to decide if you need everything you want or if you should just stick to the essentials this week. Another example would be purchasing a car or a house through a loan. You will often find yourself deciding whether to **apply for a loan from this bank** or **go to another, which** offers a lower interest rate and more facilities.

Whatever the situation, we are all exposed to the basic accounting principles every day, and your decisions are just a smaller version of those a business owner must make.

Those basic principles include:

- Gathering financial information from various sources.
- Considering all known factors before deciding.
- Deciding and evaluating it occasionally.

What is Accounting?

Fundamentally, you are acting as your own accountant in many life situations. This lets you sometimes choose or find a much better deal when facing shortfalls in your budget or simply when you prefer to make expenditure cuts when your cash flow is tight.

Accounting revolves not only around the concept of cash or monetary wealth, but it also revolves around other fundamental areas that involve:

- Risk analysis and risk management
- Opportunity cost and decision making
- Optimal solutions for various problems etc.

Thus, in simple terms, accounting is:

"THE ANALYSIS OF THE RETROSPECTIVE EVENTS MERGED WITH PRESENT VARIABLE FACTORS TO MAKE A REASONABLE ASSUMPTION/ EXPECTATION OR FORM FUTURE DECISIONS."

Although many people consider that accounting means recording past events, that is not the case. Accounting has a far broader scope in the real world, expanding to most sectors and horizons of world economies.

Does an Accountant Play a Vital Role?

The short answer is yes. Business accounting provides you, as the owner, with a detailed picture of your business. An accountant can help you track your income and expenditures, make sure you stay compliant with government and state legislation, taxes and provide you, your investors, and the government with financial information, helping you make the right business decisions.

But an accountant wears many hats, depending on the type and size of business they work for, such as:

1. Advice on Business Structures

One of the most critical accounting roles is giving advice, and much of that surrounds structuring your business in the right way. It also covers financial restructuring, corporate compliance, and these diverse areas:

- HR policies and employee enhancement programs
- Implementation of an efficient control system
- Organizational enhancement structures
- Mergers and Acquisitions
- Legal matters and dispute resolution, etc.

More accountants are also branching out into giving independent financial advice and business analysis.

2. Invoices and Billing

Every business's primary goal is to earn money. An accountant is needed to make sure every customer is billed and invoiced on a timely basis. If nobody is issuing invoices or recovering the money from customers, your business cannot succeed. An accountant is essential to oversee these processes and perform the necessary steps to handle these matters.

3. Credit Limits and Booking Sales

Businesses determine the credit limits of their customers, and these play a crucial role. **Credit limits decide how much the customer may take in goods or services rendered without paying right away.** Many businesses rely on working within their credit limits, as loans are a typical transaction when businesses are starting up. Sales are a vital part of the business's success, determining its growth and profitability potential. An accountant can easily keep a record of such sales for small businesses.

They provide a large variety of reports about small businesses, including customer reports determining who the major buyers are and who require frequent goods and services from you?

4. Supplier Invoices

An accountant's primary task is to manage the finances or manage the business's money to use it most optimally. Accountants do the particular phase of payments at the right time to make sure that a streamlined process is followed. Suppliers mostly contact the accountant of the business directly to ask about their outstanding invoices. It is the accountant's job to make sure that they are paid at the right time and that the company doesn't run out of cash. This is a vital function to keep business flowing smoothly.

5. Payroll System Management

In large businesses, HR handles the task of creating the payroll. In small businesses, the accountant mainly looks after the payroll and hiring as well. Accountants are needed to create the payroll to keep track of the employees so that no employee is overpaid or underpaid in any circumstances. If there are more than three to four employees in a business, it becomes difficult to keep track of all their payments - not to mention how much your business owes those employees. Accountants create a much-streamlined process that ensures time is recorded adequately, and no employee is left unpaid each month.

6. Legal Consultant

The laws of every country are continually changing, and this can lead to:

   • Restriction in the performance of business activities
   • Abiding by specific new rules and regulations to avoid penalties

- Evaluation of the on-going performance of business activities in the country

It is essentially a requirement to have an accountant represent you in legal matters because accountants are always up to date in their field of knowledge. This allows companies to avoid any restrictions or fines that can impair their business growth.

Do You Need an Accountant?

Small businesses rarely need an accountant to perform these tasks. It is not safe to assume that accountants are not needed, and many business owners and entrepreneurs have an accountant by their side to make sure their business runs smoothly.

When one person tries to do everything, it is too much, and the business will suffer. An accountant or bookkeeper might be needed to help with the workload while getting on with the daily business needs.

But if you are a small business owner and want to handle these aspects on a smaller scale, then your approach to handling these things on your own is feasible and cost-effective.

The key to this system is balancing your workload and making sure you don't take on too much. This will guarantee disruption is kept to a minimum, and the business can run smoothly.

Primary Tasks of an Accountant

To illustrate, please have a look at the following image:

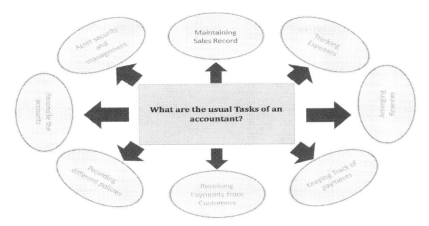

The image explains the crucial elements to help you get up to speed with what you must remember when you act as your accountant:

1. Have a proper sales record maintained.

2. Keep track of all your expenses and don't accidentally pay an invoice twice – this can happen with large businesses due to glitches in their accounting software.

3. Ensure that you have a solid policy in place and a proper contract that enforces customer payments within the timeline defined and gives no customer excessive credit. Have an appropriate credit limit for each customer and change it whenever necessary.

4. Ensure that you have proper contact with the bank so that if you ever run low on cash, the bank can provide a loan to cover the costs and keep your business going.

5. Play it safe when selecting your suppliers, as many people often place too much trust in a supplier, which they use to exploit their customers and increase their prices. So always look for different quotes and weigh them up before making a decision.

6. Make sure that security is in place to protect your valuables. This can include cash, vehicles, or high-value inventory, which can be easily pocketed or stolen.

Chapter 2: Accounting Vs. Bookkeeping

In the previous chapter, we learned about accounting and what being an accountant means. This chapter will unveil the common differences between accounting and bookkeeping, giving you a snapshot of what each handles.

Is Accounting Different from Bookkeeping?

You may come across these terms and think that accounting and bookkeeping are the same things, but we assure you they are not. To explain why, consider that bookkeeping is like a slice of a pizza, whereas accounting is the whole pizza.

Bookkeeping is a small slice of the larger pie, a small part of accounting, whereas accounting has a much more comprehensive and broader scope.

We can take this to another level. Accounting is summarized into five major components, and the following flowchart will provide a lot of value to your understanding.

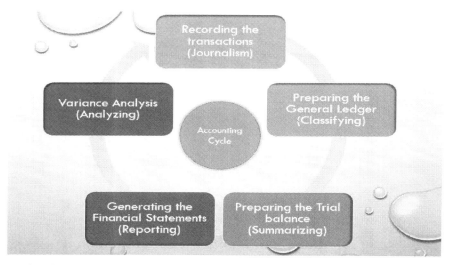

So here we can see that accounting combines its sub-divided components:

1. Record the Transactions

This component involves recording the financial transactions which have occurred. This is a crucial technique to ensure that all data is captured and considered for necessary processing. Every accountant ensures that the data or transaction, which they record, has all the necessary details and meets all the necessary criteria to prove the data's adequacy. This first step plays a significant role in three key areas:

a) An integrated control system that perfectly captures all required data.

b) Surety in the continuity of the business's financial strength.

c) Reporting at the final stage.

2. Classifying the Recorded Transactions

Once the data is captured and recorded, the next phase involves classifying those transactions into various headings, according to what the transaction pertains to. Examples include office furniture, business vehicle expenditure, stock, sales, and so on.

3. Summarize the Entire Record

Summarization means using all the data found in every category or class and putting it together to form a complete information set. Summarization is the first processing phase, displaying a brief but concise financial picture.

4. Report the Information

Most business owners want several reports, allowing them to analyze different facets of their business. That can be done only if the initial data is sufficient, so if the data captured at the primary stages lacked solid ground and detail, the final reports would not be complete. The most important report is the profit/loss statement, showing the business's financial standings quickly.

5. Analyze the Information

Even though the information may seem organized and easy to understand, it can be far from it. Much of this comes down to who collected and processed the information and how good the records were. If proper records are not kept, it may be impossible for a third-party, such as a bookkeeper, to understand them. Information analysis involves matching the information to previous years, providing an idea of whether the business has grown or not and how successfully, or otherwise.

10 Major Differences Between Bookkeeping and Accounting

To clarify the difference between the two, we have placed a side-by-side comparison table, illustrating this better.

	Accounting	Bookkeeping
Scope	We have elaborated on how it considers all five components to form a single scope in accounting. But its major work acts out on interpretation, analyzing, and reporting the financial information.	Bookkeeping is typically involved in the identification, measurement, and recording of financial events. That's why bookkeeping is a part of accounting.
Data Processing	Accounting involves heavily extensive data processing, as every single part of the data obtained has to be reported in a concise and meaningful manner.	There is no data processing in bookkeeping as it only captures the data, records it, and provides safekeeping of data collection.

Management's Decisions	Accounting is the primary tool used by the management for decision-making. Accounting is further divided into two main areas that include cost and management accounting and financial accounting. Management uses both of accounting for their respective uses and needs.	Bookkeeping doesn't allow management to form decisions or make valuable decisions based on the data gathered, as raw data provides no insight into how it reflects the overall process unless it is processed adequately.
Use in Purpose	Accounting's use or purpose is primarily for management and third parties to obtain valuable information about its operations.	Bookkeeping's use and purpose is to capture and record financial events adequately.
Competency Required	Accounting requires competent people to form reports, and analyzing the data is complex and complicated.	Bookkeeping doesn't require competency as it is followed in a systematic and pre-designed manner.
Categories	Accounting is further divided into categories for management use. (Explained above)	Bookkeeping is divided into two systems. Single-entry systems or dual entry systems.

Report Preparation	Various reports and financial statements are prepared at the end of the accounting procedure.	Bookkeeping doesn't involve the preparation of any such statements.
Analyze the Information	Accounting involves an extensive analysis of the information, which only well-trained people can do due to the complexity of the task's nature.	It includes no analysis of the information.
Qualifications	The necessary qualifications for a person to be a competent accountant include being either a CA (Chartered Accountant), ACCA (Association of Chartered Certified Accountant), CPA (Certified Public Accountant), CMA (Cost and Management Accountant), etc.	Any person can perform bookkeeping with any qualifications.
Level of Experience	Accounting requires a great level of experience.	Bookkeeping requires no experience as it is easy to perform.

Modern Day Bookkeeping and Accounting

In modern times, both fields have experienced massive changes and shifts in their scope and line of work. With introducing semi-automatic processing and AI (Artificial Intelligence), the world around accounting and bookkeeping quickly evolved to cope with ever-changing technology.

Experts estimate that the accounting business will be valued at almost $12 billion by 2026. Now, most small businesses and startups consider the accountant one of the most critical parts of their organization. That might seem like a surprising statistic, but the main factor in all this is that organizations realize the bookkeeper's importance, help a business streamline operations, and manage their finances. A good bookkeeper can make life a little easier for the accountant, allowing them to produce accurate reports at the right times to make sure of compliance and to process tax filings when due.

The Emergence of Accounting and Bookkeeping Software

The never-ending changes in technology led to the combination of both accounting and bookkeeping software and software such as QuickBooks, SAAP, and Sage50, which combined both processes. Once the data is entered and punched into the system, the software automatically displays all the reports, eliminating the effort to classify, summarize, and report data and go straight to recording the transactions and then receiving the desired reports. These reports also give a detailed analysis and review of the financial information.

Efficient and Economic Services

Due to these rapid changes, many services accountants traditionally offered became extraordinarily competitive and cheap. This made multiple services such as bookkeeping, tax preparation, and financial statement analysis cheaper to prepare when individually offered or even as a whole. As more consistency and integrity were found in the information that companies could produce, people didn't need help from accountants. The same set of information needed for official and governmental purposes was easily produced.

Financial Literacy and Ease in Processes

World modernization has led to more people being financially literate. Many people who used to find bookkeeping and accounting a difficult task now find it easier to adapt. These days, most retail stores, restaurants, even coffee shops' built-in integrated system takes the order and keeps track of the inventory and the sales made per order. This has led to more people being aware of the need to be financially literate and make the right business decisions to succeed.

Introduction of New Services

Remote working has never been easier. High-speed internet, cloud-based computing, and online databases have made it possible to work from just about anywhere globally, which has helped to introduce a new line of services offered by bookkeepers and accountants. A bookkeeper can work from anywhere, as they have access to decent internet, which has led to a surge in outsourcing. Business owners can now hire a bookkeeper online, using freelancer agencies, outsourcing agencies, and simple online advertising. Parts of the business easy to outsource include:

- Payroll processing systems and online payroll management systems
- Credit Card and Debit card processing systems
- Reconciliation of the financial transactions
- Tax calculation and tax-related services
- Internal control management systems, etc.

These services have allowed many companies and small businesses to increase their profitability and ease the processes. And freelancers can access the work from anywhere in the world.

Besides all this, even accountants have enhanced their level of services, including:

- Financial advisory and risk assessment advisory
- Budgeting and resource management
- Financial analyst and forecasting, etc.

The Future Reality of Bookkeeping and Accounting

After learning how bookkeeping and accounting have merged, you realize what the future holds in both fields. It is an unarguable fact that soon AI (Artificial Intelligence) will take over the entire process of bookkeeping and accounting. As machines automatically capture and record transactions, less human interaction will be involved in the entire process.

The most useful service, which will stay afloat regardless of AI introduction, will be financial analysis and resource allocation. Auditing will also stay in existence due to its regulatory status. Otherwise, bookkeeping will become obsolete shortly.

Key Tips to Select the Perfect Bookkeeping Software

When selecting the bookkeeping and accounting software, follow these essential tips:

1. Select the software that offers the perfect compatibility for your use. If you are a service industry, you select the software that offers the best accounting for service businesses.

2. Remember to stay consistent when inputting data into your systems, as it is an essential daily chore to follow.

3. Don't be afraid to change the software if you feel the current one doesn't fulfill your requirements.

4. Follow the key instructions and guidelines that come with each software so you can navigate better.

5. Remember to buy the software that offers security and protection against unauthorized entry, as your records are also precious and crucial to your business.

6. Keep a good habit of having several backups of the records and make sure you have an indexed physical record to navigate easily.

Chapter 3: Which Accounting Methods Suit My Small Business?

In the previous chapters, we explained the primary ideas and concepts about accounting and how it differs from bookkeeping. In this section, we will cover the following core ideas:

- The need for accounting methods and their essential types
- The crucial need for accounting methods in business entities
- Core benefits of each type of system. And most importantly
- How would this provide a direct benefit to you as a small business owner?

Do I Need an Accounting Method?

You may hear many accountants use the term "accounting methods" and wonder what accounting methods are? For the ease of your understanding, an accounting method is how you handle your accounts or financial records. Typically, financial records aren't the only things considered for accounting methods: non-financial records, events, or aspects can directly play in financial transactions. Don't worry about this, as this doesn't concern you. It is briefly defined here to elaborate on what can constitute a financial record.

You need an accounting method for your small business. You need this because:

>1. Accounting methods create an easy way to identify the natural aspect of reporting your business.

>2. It creates ease in understanding how your business performs with variable changing factors.

>3. It allows your business to realize and recognize revenue and thus report accurate or adequate profits.

At this point, you may be wondering whether you need to decide upon an accounting method, but you may also wonder what all this means.

Accrual or Cash - What are These Accounting Methods?

Usually, the accounting methods are categorized into two:

>1. Cash method of accounting

>2. Accrual method of accounting

Cash Method

The cash method of accounting involves recording all the financial transactions based on the amount of cash received or cash spent during a particular period. This includes the cash received or spent in the form of banking transactions or cash in hand.

Small business owners mostly use the cash method of accounting, as it is easy to maintain and needs the physical cash to be present for use. For business taxes and preparation of the financial records, it is essential to remember that the primary selection of a method at the start can have huge risks or rewards associated with it.

To further elaborate, the Cash method of accounting states:

- **Recording Physical Income** - Say you received a sum of money from a client after a particular period. The income was received on the first day of the next calendar period but was associated with the previous calendar period. This income will be logged into the next calendar period.

- **Book Paid Expenses** - Say that the salaries of the employees in December 2018 were paid in January 2019. The expense would be recorded in January 2019.

Accrual Method

This method of accounting involves recording revenue with associated expenses or vice versa. This also means that revenue or expense related to a particular period must be recorded in the same period rather than recording when received or paid.

This method follows the accounting principle of the **Matching Concept** that states that:

- **Revenue - It must be recorded when we receive it.** For instance, you have supplied goods or services to a customer and sent an invoice in January 2019 but received the payment in February 2019. Here, your revenue must be logged in January 2019.

- **Expenses - Must be logged when we pay them.** For instance, salaries of the staff for January 2019 were paid in February 2019. As these salaries relate to January 2019, they should have been recorded at that time.

The Accrual accounting method follows a unique composure of accounting entries involving the right to receive, or a right to receive is established. Our revenue must be logged along with a corresponding asset, termed as a receivable.

The same case applies that when we must pay, or when it is established that we must pay for a service or goods received, we book our expenses and correspondingly book a liability, i.e., an obligation by the business to pay.

The fundamental idea of the matching concept leads many businesses to consider the accrual method of accounting.

5 Pros and Cons to Know Which Method Suits You the Best

Cash Method - Pros

The cash method has these pros:

1. Bookkeeping is Simple and Comparatively Easy

Maintaining your records based on cash is easy, and it keeps the records in a streamlined manner. The entire bookkeeping process becomes simple. There should never be any concern that income and expenses have not been included in the system, particularly those that should be logged. As everything will get reconciled at the end of a certain period, the idea that income or expenses will be missed or left unrecorded won't be an issue. It doesn't mean that invoices or bills won't be generated, as all bookkeeping records will eventually generate invoices or bills to display that these match with the cash received or spent.

2. Accurate Cash Flow Tracks

As everything is maintained in the form of cash at hand or cash in the bank, every point of the accounting system displays and tells you how much cash can be used and how much financing will be needed to sustain any future activity. This also provides the perfect indicator of the cash strength of a business.

3. Easy to Reconcile the Cash Using the Records

Not only that, but this method also allows business owners to reconcile any differences that arise during their work in a shorter period. Since transactions can be traced through the actual amount of cash, it makes the small business owner's work easy, especially if all cash transactions were recorded when they happened.

4. No Need for an Accountant or Advisor

With the immense flexibility and easy understanding of the method, there is no need for an expert-level accountant or advisor to be employed, thus saving money. You can easily perform the task of maintaining the records yourself and have it done relatively quickly, so long as you record everything regularly and don't leave it all to the end of the month.

5. Cost-Effective and Cheap to Sustain

The best advantage of the method is that it is extremely cost-effective. Along with that, this entire method saves time and resources to focus on more crucial work rather than having to spend countless hours fixing accounting records or errors.

Disadvantages

As with anything, there are always disadvantages that offset the benefits in different situations.

1. Unclear Picture About the Performance of the Business

This is one of the most significant downsides of the cash method. To show you what I mean, let me give you an example. For instance, your business performs its activities in the construction sector. You must have financing (a loan) to start the work before receiving the house's construction payments (after three years). If you go to a bank or any financial institution and ask for a loan, they will likely reject your application because you have not received a cash payment for doing the construction, and you have yet to record any revenue for the project. This is the case until the end of the project, and the bank will not consider this until the money is paid. Without finance or a loan, you won't be able to construct the house, and thus you will receive no revenue.

This example depicts the vicious cycle in which small business owners can get stuck while adopting the cash method. It creates an unclear image of business performance and the business's ability to continue. Not only that:

- It shows the business's poor performance if the business earns revenue in a single season and not over a more extended period.

- It depicts that the business has immense losses when the significant financing or loans are eventually paid back to the financial institutions.

- It categorizes the business as high risk with high rewards, which many shareholders or investors are unwilling to take.

2. Disturbance in Tracking Profit Each Month

Another big drawback of this method is calculating the profit after the period. For instance, if you didn't pay the salaries or warehouse rent for a particular month, it would be difficult to know the actual profit for that month. Not only that, but this insecurity also makes it harder to perform any analysis.

3. Misreporting and Improper Basis for Comparison

This method relies heavily on when the cash is paid, creating a gateway for people to misuse and misreport the facts and figures. Typically, small business owners manipulate the figures by delaying payments or simply avoiding recording such payments as cash-in-hand transactions are the least likely to be well documented. This creates two major issues:

- This method is well known among investors, making them less likely to invest in your business if it follows such a method.

- A comparison of such records is impossible due to the volatile behavior that the business portrays.

4. Harder to Keep track of Receivables and Payables

Most businesses rely on credit terms, allowing them to manage their finances and cash flows better. In the cash accounting method, the concept of receivables and payables doesn't exist. That's why many small business owners have to keep a separate record of such transactions, which is harder to maintain and follow.

5. Inaccurate Forecasts

As many risks associated with the businesses involve revenue recognition and understatement of expenses, this causes inaccurate forecasts about the business's performance.

Pros in the Use of Accrual Method

Standard business practices include using the accrual accounting method because of the wide range of benefits.

1. More Optimized Track Record

The best pro-benefit of using the accrual method is that it tracks the operational performance much better. Recording all the transactions at the date of occurrence allows the business owner to analyze the business and its working conditions better.

2. Increase Third-Party Trust and Reliability

As the business creates a more unified and well-mannered form of reporting and financial statements, it increases its credibility. This allows third parties such as investors to invest in the business or banks to provide loans and finances and build a better client reputation and a diverse portfolio.

3. Accounting for Every Single Transaction

The best part about accrual-based accounting is that every aspect of the business is properly recorded, documented, and passed through the system to ensure everything is in order. Not only that, but it also gives the best idea about the receivables and payables of the business and is more transparent.

4. Accurate Profitability Each Month

The Accrual method of accounting provides accurate profitability margins at the end of each period or month-end. This makes the company perform monthly or periodic analysis by comparing the figures with the previous year to understand its performance.

In the earlier instance, it was described that for a construction sector business, the ability to take up loans is practically impossible while following the cash method. That issue gets resolved easily by the accrual method of accounting.

5. Easy Analysis and Forecasts

Many accountants can create well-designed reports and forecasts, which accurately depict the business's future in the upcoming months. Large entities have a highly skilled profile of expert accountants present in large numbers who constantly monitor and examine its growth in the forthcoming periods. It can also become easy for small businesses, as many factors are already available, and it can be easily forecasted whether the business will survive.

Cons of Accrual Method

Even though the accrual method may seem outstanding and the best to adopt, it also has cons, making it incompatible for certain people.

1. Difficult to Track Cash Flow Issues

All businesses need to understand the cash they have to use for various financial activities. Tracing cash flow is comparatively easy in the accrual method, but the problems within those said cash flows are hard to determine. The main reason is when the financial statements follow the accrual method, they consider non-cash items/ transactions and even those that haven't been cashed in or out. The best example of this is the same construction industry, which has taken a loan and based its activities on the accrual method. Now the company might be depicting hefty profits and incurring costs, but, in reality, there is no physical presence of cash, and their account could be standing at a zero balance.

2. It Can Be Expensive and Complex

The accrual method has a complicated design to follow to provide optimal results and reports. Since these designs have to be in place within a proper control system, it sometimes becomes expensive to maintain or sustain such designs. Larger companies and businesses' gigantic network integrates humans with machines to produce accurate and non-collusive results. These designs, which have to be in place, sometimes cost a lot of money and are so complicated they need consistent help from experts.

3. Stay up to Date with New Laws

One big issue about the accrual method is that all accountants or business owners must continuously stay in touch with new accounting standards and the new laws. You would need to know new accounting standards because they always affect the existing laws. All business owners need to understand and enforce them.

4. More Money Means More Tax

Let's take the same example of the construction industry business where the person is earning high profits due to adopting the accrual method. Since their financial statements show profits, they would have to pay taxes on the profit earned. From the previous example explanation, they don't have the money to pay tax as there has been no money received until now.

This is precisely why the accrual method makes people pay more taxes in one particular period and then fewer taxes in another. This makes it more complicated for business owners to understand how these tax laws affect their financial performance.

5. The Constant Need for an Expert

You will need an accountant's help often because working as an administrator or banker is an intensive routine. Not only that, but accountants will also only solve such matters they are trained to handle when dealing with complex or unknown issues or cases. Thus, this increases the cost of handling the accounts and the accrual method.

Which Method is Perfect for You?

Now the real question that arises – what accounting method will suit my company the best? You may have noticed that each method has pros and cons.

Here are ways to best relate to your situation, helping you choose the most suitable method for your business. For instance, if you are a small business owner and want to run an independent business with no accountants or you are a business accountant, the **cash method of accounting** would suit you the best. The reason is that:

   0• You may want to save costs and not have a large amount of time invested in accounting records or maintaining financial records. Or

   1• You may incur a cost, but your business direction or the business motive is to handle a more cash-based profit, so cash flow problems or reconciliations do not arise.

You can also adopt the accrual method based on the pros and cons you read in the last section. The method selection is weighted on three factors:

   1. Business structure or business motive.

   2. Resource utilization.

   3. Reporting requirements.

Suppose your company follows a strict pattern or line where significant revenues are seasonal or period-based, or your company heavily relies on the reporting requirements to track business requirements better. There, the **accrual method** is perfect for your needs. As you know from the accrual method downsides, one of the main things to look out for is the cost and the necessity of such reports.

As a small business owner, you may not face such requirements of needing a high reporting line. Still, if you are a stable business and want to expand further, then the accrual method will depict your business's actual position and performance so it can expand further. Hence, if you start your business from the basics, adopt the cash method to ease the entire process.

Almost everywhere, regulatory bodies allow a business to shift from one method to another. The safe and secure approach uses both methods when you feel it is the right time to adopt that method.

Getting Into the Systems: Single Entry or Double Entry

The detailing of your chosen method gives you direction. Whether you want to perform record maintenance daily, weekly, or monthly, there is bound to be a method you can follow easily because, inherently, you will need to keep track of references before properly maintaining the financial records.

Suppose you are caught up in daily work and don't have time to compile all the transactions into proper records. What would be your approach to making sure that today's transactions aren't forgotten by tomorrow? You might typically note them down in a rough manner somewhere as a reminder. That is how the accounting systems work. They are based on the idea that the data written into the transaction's record is incomplete and written roughly – or written in full detail by reflecting on its appropriate nature.

Partial System: Single Entries

Just as the name describes it, it is a partial system. This system is only partial because it doesn't consider the level of accounting needed. Most transactions are maintained roughly or partially, with little information present about each transaction. This system is relatively easy and simple, but things get a little more difficult when processing it into the correct classes or groups.

A single-entry system primarily controls the cash received and the cash spent. It doesn't consider the inventory, the receivables, and the payables in the system. Remember that this system is not the perfect match for the cash method. Because many people maintain a single-entry system employing the accrual method, it facilitates performing control evaluations.

How Does this System Work?

This system works like a small cash statement. For instance, in a cash statement, there are two columns. In the right column, write the amount of cash and any other income received, while in the left column, write all the expenses and anything else that reduces our cash reserves. This is much like a personal record book that allows you to maintain partial information about each transaction. This is commonly done by many people when recording partial information in their checkbooks.

What this system doesn't correctly maintain is the *balance sheet information,* such as assets or liabilities. Many people use them as control measures to reassess their entire assets or liabilities under the accrual method. This approach is sometimes misleading and can lead to fraudulent activities taking place.

The General Accepted Accounting Principles (GAAP) don't recommend following the single-entry approach – even for small businesses – because of that very reason. Because it is easy to record transactions, many people opt to continue this to save time and resources.

The Complete System: Double Entry System

Almost every SME (Small Medium Enterprise) business and large businesses follow the modern world's double-entry accounting system. It is a popular method because it keeps the entire system of accounting well maintained and balanced. Common practices and principles are also based on the double-entry system because it provides a more secure and well-balanced approach to maintaining the accounts.

The main reason this system is so popular is that it prevents multiple errors and other mistakes from taking place and allows you to prevent common mistakes, which can sometimes become harder to detect.

How Does this System Perform?

This system's central concept is that every transaction has two effects, opposite to one another; there will always be an increasing impact while, simultaneously, there will also be a decreasing impact. Such impacts give an overall equilibrium, and the equation is always balanced. These two balancing natures of the transactions are called *debit* and *credit.*

The concepts regarding debit and credit may seem misguided. We can simplify the inaccurate accounting concept by saying that some account elements are debits, and some are credits. That's not to say that debit elements cannot also occur as a credit and vice versa.

We will not go into detail about the accounting equation here, but it is essential to explain it briefly to help you understand. We'll cover this more broadly in an upcoming chapter.

These natures of debit and credit fall into the direct criteria of the accounting equation, which is:

ASSETS = LIABILITIES + OWNER'S EQUITY

whereby

ASSETS (Debit nature) = LIABILITIES + OWNERS'S EQUITY (Credit nature)

From the equation, we can see that assets primarily have a debit nature while liabilities or owners' equity has a credit nature. Thus, whenever an asset (say the purchase of a vehicle occurred in this transaction) increases, this will be considered a debit. If it is caused by a liability (say a bank loan was taken, so the bank name should be titled in the transaction), then the credit effect becomes one of liability.

This entire transaction will be depicted like this:

Vehicle A/C (An Asset)   Dr. 10,000

To Bank Loan- BOA A/C (A Liability)   Cr. 10,000

This transaction reflects the equally balanced equation on the purchase of an asset with liability. If the reduction of another asset causes it (say you purchased the vehicle with cash in hand or cash at the bank), that asset will have an equal credit effect, reducing the asset.

For example:

Vehicle A/C (An Asset)   Dr. 10,000

To Cash at Bank A/C   Cr. 10,000

(The symbol A/C means account.) Here in these transactions, we have seen how debit and credit natures play a role in the double-entry accounting system, which is not found in the single-entry system.

Common Differences to Help You Understand Both Systems

To clear up any misconceptions or misunderstandings you may have, we will provide the differences between both systems, as follows.

- The impartial system of single entry only records one side of the transaction, a debit or a credit. The complete mechanism of the double-entry system records both effects for a balanced approach.

- The impartial system is relatively simple and easy to handle, whereas the double-entry system is comparatively harder to maintain and sometimes becomes complex to handle.

- The impartial system doesn't produce accurate and complete records, while the other system produces accurate and error-free results in most cases.

- It is easy to detect and trace any errors or risks of fraudulent activities in the double-entry system. In contrast, the impartial system offers no technique that can help trace fraudulent activities.

- The best and most accurate comparison of the two periods can be made only with the balanced system rather than the single-entry system. The latter doesn't provide a good record-maintenance technique.

In the following chapters, we'll focus on all techniques and learning methodologies in the double-entry system with the accrual method as this system is complex to handle. Unless specified, we will explain the cash method when working with the systems.

Chapter 4: Ten Tools for Digital Accounting

This section of the chapter will focus on accounting software and its need in modern times. Essentially this chapter will cover:

- The different types of accounting software and use in the technological era

- The key differences between various software

- The benefit various software will provide you with according to your business model

This chapter will typically cover the different software that businesses use. We will try to keep the information as relatable to you as possible.

Digital Software of the 21st Century

Ever since technology entered our lives, almost every single aspect of life has been transformed. Most technologies are designed to help us save time, making life simpler and more efficient. Most people embrace technology these days. Even in accounting, digital software has made remarkable breakthroughs, allowing millions of consumers to do their work more easily while dedicating time to their businesses' more crucial aspects.

Many current accounting software packages have hugely affected how large and small businesses can control their finances. The most common software packages popular among the small businesses are:

- QuickBooks Online
- Sage Accounting
- Xero
- Sage 300
- FreshBooks
- WagePoint
- SurePayroll
- TSheets
- Expensify
- Neat

Being an entrepreneur is challenging, and during these challenging times, it is also essential to manage your business efficiently. Trying to manage every aspect of your business is hard, especially for keeping track of your finances while ensuring everything else runs smoothly. Luckily, most accounting software makes life easier. While it won't do everything for you, it can take the brunt of the work, making it a real game-changer for almost every business.

1. QuickBooks Online

Starting with one of the most popular accounting tools, QuickBooks Online has emerged as a game-changing software that provided ease in the workplace. With simple invoicing to record handling and tracking payments, QuickBooks does it all while you sit back, relax, and enjoy a cup of coffee and watch your business boom in the market. Most business owners don't have the time to spend on their financial records to make sure their business runs smoothly.

Luckily QuickBooks Online saves you from much of the work and even produces reports on late-paying customers. And if you are worried that QuickBooks Online might not be adaptive to your business model, don't be because it has a vast range of built-in databases that suit many users.

QuickBooks also allows you to pre-load your custom invoice template rather than relying on standard designs in the system. With the considerable diversity in the reporting and the advanced reporting functionalities offered by QuickBooks, you won't have to invest time in preparing reports either.

With the automatic sync features, QuickBooks integrates your bank statements or credit card e-statements and processes them instantly. In short, QuickBooks help you manage just about every financial aspect of your business.

2. Sage Accounting

Following the same popularity as QuickBooks Online, Sage Accounting also benefits you and your company. This accounting software typically handles the project management features and other features related to particular jobs. By providing accurate costing and cost allocation to jobs, this software helps entrepreneurs to trace their cash-flow and manage their profits on every project. By covering the project management side, this software plays a significant role in the service industries that typically rely on each project's cash generation.

Not only that, but Sage Accounting also applies further enhancements by displaying the best functionality margins for your business. Considering the standard costs, it displays results showing you where money can be saved. Although it requires some input level to generate estimated results, it is more efficient.

As an entrepreneur, if you feel that your business model has more projects and project costs have a vital role in performance, Sage Accounting will help. Even though QuickBooks Online provides an enhanced costing mechanism, as a beginner, Sage Accounting makes the process easy and detailed so you can understand it easily.

3. Xero

With major competitors such as QuickBooks Online, Xero also upholds a prominent reputation in the market. Although resembling QuickBooks in many features, this accounting software has unique features to offer to its clients. Unlike QuickBooks, Xero has more integrated security features that let it leave QuickBooks Online behind. Even though this is the case, Xero lacks many features that QuickBooks offers but can produce plenty of reports, all customized and varying from industry to industry.

It also gives the primary user the ability to create many other users to speed up the operational work. If you are running a small business, you might need more users to log into the software. If your business has multiple divisions on a small to medium scale, then the integrated feature to include people from the different divisions may prove beneficial.

As an entrepreneur, you know everything about your business model. As the market reputation matters a lot, it is essential to know what values your business aims to target. Keeping this in mind, you may want to tap into a new market to spread your business values. Thus, Xero will prove to be the most efficient and cost-effective accounting software to meet your purpose or to meet your particular requirements in such a case.

4. Sage 300

The most advanced use of any software lies in cloud-based systems, where every piece of data is stored and saved. Sage 300 offers the same benefit to its customers by ensuring that every aspect of your business is secured and out of harm's way. The cloud allows your business's financial records to be accessed from anywhere in the world. It has the edge on making sure that your work is streamlined and isn't restricted.

With the standard features, just like Sage Accounting, Sage 300 provides a more secure and integrated line of reporting and maintaining financial records. You may be putting your data and records at risk of being exposed or used by unauthorized users or hackers. Keeping the data inaccessible and not stored on physical hardware at your premises, security is much tighter.

Not only that, but a cloud-based system also allows the information and data to be accessed from anywhere by anyone with permission easily, and it offers a faster recovery time. Invoice generation, payroll, sales, and other facilities make it easier to track any division's performance at any time from any place safely.

5. FreshBooks

Like QuickBooks, FreshBooks has gained popularity, offering various features embedded in its centralized system. FreshBooks allows for full control of the systematic design for you with its consistency and record maintaining abilities. The integration and security features also resemble QuickBooks and Xero. With the integrated CRM and customer track records system, FreshBooks serves all your financial needs.

Being an entrepreneur, you need to know how your customer revenues are maintained and how they can play a vital role in determining your business's goodwill. FreshBooks also offers customer support services to ensure that every client is satisfied and there is no disruption in your company's everyday operations. You must always keep a balanced state of work for both employees and customers as both have a crucial role in your business's success.

FreshBooks offers reliability and consistency, making it a great accounting software for those who wish to have a more precise track record of their customers.

Your business management requires the necessary resources at hand to guarantee a consistent process without any failure or malfunction. Even if you run a small business, you must ensure that where operations are a crucial factor in the business, revenue streams must also be considered to create a more robust business portfolio and its working criteria.

Top Payroll Accounting Tools

As operations grow larger and larger, payroll processing is an essential part of work-related activities. Whether small or large, many businesses use various opportunities to reduce their payroll processing costs and make sure of accurate calculations to avoid any improper payments made to employees. The standard practices that most businesses use are:

- Allowing an outsourcing firm to handle payroll processing

- Making the managers keep track of the team's working hours and reporting it

- Hiring an independent third party who tracks and records employees working hours

- Creating an HR (Human Resource) department that checks the payroll

These methods and techniques are useful and beneficial, allowing many business owners to save necessary resources (either time or cost) and keep everything in order. Even as an entrepreneur, you can easily save time and cost without investing so much money with payroll processing software.

1. WagePoint

A comparatively simple and easy tool to use, WagePoint provides all the essential benefits and uses of payroll processing software. By keeping track of the time and the hours charged in its timesheets, WagePoint essentially becomes an easy tool to use. This not only helps you save yourself from the hectic day-to-day work, but it also ensures that every single form is processed correctly.

One of the significant features it includes, just like every other payroll processing software, ensures that taxes and other such deductions are made automatically and accurately. Is it essential for you to know how much tax needs to be paid and the number of salaries paid? If you are a small business and managing all the employees, this software is excellent for you. As a large business, this software might not be up to par as it can't trace any wrongful payment made to the employees. It doesn't provide the audit trail features that enable you to track the entire movement.

But as a small business owner, this software is suitable because of its simplicity in use and ease of understanding.

2. SurePayroll

Following the same features of WagePoint, SurePayroll offers an even more straightforward and easier version to use without advanced tools or mechanisms. This software is typically used by small business owners who prefer to keep things manageable while ensuring that the entire process follows a smooth and consistent method. This software has no advanced mechanism or automatic time tracking system. It does calculate the tax accurately, ensuring you don't face the consequences of incorrect declarations.

Not only that, but SurePayroll also lives up to its name and makes sure that the payroll is completed powered in the most precise manner possible. Without disrupting or causing problems in any daily tasks, SurePayroll provides every sort of report you may need.

Top Time Tracking and Expense Software

When we talk about payroll processing, the core factor that makes your payroll accurate is time. Many of you may already know that time tracking is a significant factor because no business wants to overpay or underpay their workers. The biggest problem with time tracking is that it causes the payments to change even if there may only have been a single-digit error in punching in the time. To ensure that no such errors or mistakes occur, and every process is followed, here are the best time tracking software packages available.

1. TSheets

One of the best time tracking software packages on the market, TSheets gives its users remarkable features and benefits. By creating a dynamic system where tasks and project confusion are minimized, TSheets integrates your employees' best productivity. By ensuring that everything passes through the series of procedures, TSheets makes it remarkably easy to use and becomes top-of-the-line.

It also allows people to track their time no matter where they are in the world and keep the process streamlined for everyone to understand. TSheets is commonly used for QuickBooks Online and Xero, which integrates time tracking with the accounting systems. By optimizing the work task, TSheets provides various alerts and updates about any tasks or projects.

TSheets can be a bit expensive for you if you are trying to save costs as its cost increases for every user added to the system, but to create a better-managed control system on time tracking, then the increase in cost may be worth it for the problems it can solve. Not only that, but the entire data is stored online so you can process the time at the end of each day by confirming whether the same reconciles with the work limits.

2. Expensify

As the name suggests, this software is generally responsible for taking up the record of expenses incurred. With its scanning features, Expensify takes the records of all the receipts at hand. Being an entrepreneur, you may come across various moments when you won't have the time to upload the reports and images of the day-to-day expenses that occurred. With Expensify, this will all be made easy and a hassle-free task.

This software also works on mobiles, which allows the best use and gives you a more up-to-date status of your expenses. This also gives employees and staff convenience to upload their bills easily and create a reimbursable status for those bills.

3. Neat

Working with the same features as Expensify, Neat works in the same manner and allows its user to scan their transaction receipts. The scanning feature of Neat also functions on Mobile Devices or ordinary scanners to take up the financial data and process it. By sharing the information and details with other people, Neat becomes a handy tool to make everyday tasks easy.

Tips to Help You Select Digital Software

As you can see, there are plenty of accounting software packages that everyone around the world uses, but as a small business owner, keep the following in mind:

i. Only use the authentic version of the software as sometimes people try to scam and steal your data through fake websites and fake apps.

ii. Remember to keep a consistent backup of all financial information in a separate place to your software so it can easily be traced back or recovered with no problems.

iii. Never use cracked versions of software - always purchase an official copy. Using cracked software is not only illegal, but you also run a high risk of losing your financial data or, even worse, being hacked. If you lose your data in this way, you likely will not recover it again.

iv. Always have secure login and password on your computer and the software you are using, which will help prevent unauthorized breaches in the system.

v. Have software with a built-in function of audit trail that explains which user entered the system and what changes were made on the system.

vi. Don't ever hesitate to contact the software's customer support as they will provide you with the desired help you may seek.

vii. Be sure always to create a separate user account if someone else wants to access the data but be careful not to authorize them to access every aspect of the business.

These tips are important to learn and note, as many people commonly make these mistakes when using this accounting software for the first time.

Chapter 5: Setting Up the Charts of Accounts

In this chapter, we will look at the practicalities of setting up and using the chart of accounts. We will cover:

- What the chart of accounts is

- How the chart of accounts play a role in your work

- Setting up the chart of accounts according to your needs

- Making sure that the framework stays consistent and flexible

Let's begin.

What is the Chart of Accounts?

Any accountant who knows his stuff and has excellent advisory skills will ask a potential client one question – "What is your business model?" They want to know your income and expenditure, how you categorize them, and where your business is headed. Almost every single qualitative aspect of the real world has been quantified due to accounting. The same case applies here that your revenues or costs and your business assets have been quantified, explaining the overall business model.

This illustration was given to create a better understanding of what your business model can be defined as. Before the working business model of your company, the financial numbers played a significant role. According to their nature, these numbers need to be categorized in a pre-designed framework that integrated the entire system.

Thus, the understanding of the Chart of Accounts comes into being. The chart of accounts is the framework model of your business model's quantified aspects. Every business model has common elements, which are the core basics of accounting. Every business has:

1. Revenue/ Income

2. Expenses/ Costs

3. Assets

4. Liabilities

5. Equity

These are definitive quantified aspects of your business model, which are integrated within the financial framework known as the chart of accounts. These charts of accounts give a straight understanding of the elements that fall under them. For example, revenue is a generalized term or category defining what it means, but for a service industry business, their chart of accounts will define revenue or income as revenue from customers or contracts or Income from Contract clients, etc.

Vital Role of Chart of Accounts

The Chart of Accounts plays a crucial role in the business as these are the main foundations of your financial statements and other reports, which are generated from here on. You may think that the Chart of Accounts can be created on a general aspect with a little difference depending on the company. However, these always vary from industry to industry. They even differ from business to business in the *same industry*. And you need to know what it is and how to set them up yourself.

Besides all this, the Chart of Accounts is often specialized in a new type of industry whose business model doesn't exist right now. For instance, many startup companies' new and innovative ideas drive them to develop new and improved versions of their businesses. The nature of that business must be known if it is quantified, as it may be a business that doesn't already exist.

Usually, this can be done only by a professional, so understanding how they work is critical if you must do it yourself.

Getting Into the Practical Work: The Chart of Accounts

Before we explain how to set up the chart of accounts, a quick reminder: we will not be going into the details for each software product, but we will explain where it can be navigated from in most cases.

As earlier explained, the Chart of Accounts is a financial framework that quantifies your business model into the financial statements. It is also an indexing system that allows you to navigate your accounting elements with ease. This indexing is mostly considered in number sequences.

1. Assets

The Chart of Accounts mostly starts with the assets. Assets are all those items you may control and receive future economic benefits. These assets start with a number sequence of "1," extended to "1000," where the numbers are allotted as "1000" or "1010" or "1020". This "1000" series is commonly allotted to current assets of cash in hand or cash in the bank, commonly called *Cash* and *Cash Equivalents*. Current assets also include stock in trade, accounts receivables, Deposits, Prepayments, and other receivables. If your business is a service industry, you may not need to set up the chart of accounts for inventory as you may sell services rather than goods.

The "1000" series is allocated as a whole sequence to current assets, which will probably increase. This all depends on you because you are responsible for setting up your chart of accounts, but it does explain standard market practices. If you don't need a particular Chart of Account, you need not include or create it on your list. This entire process is subjective and depends on your requirements.

Fixed assets of Non-Current assets typically have a life span of more than one year and provide benefits over the years. In setting up the chart of accounts of fixed assets or non-current assets, they are allocated to the series sequence of "2000", which can be "2000 for Land and Buildings", "2010 for Vehicles and Automobiles", "2020 for Office Equipment and Furniture" etc.

2. Liabilities

The term liabilities are amounts we owe or simply the obligation by us to pay. In the Chart of Accounts Framework, most liabilities are given the sequence of 3, which of "3000 to 3999". Standard market practices create a considerable gap between each series. This is because new elements or forms of interpretations from the IFRS (International Financial Reporting Standards) or GAAP make it difficult for business owners to consider them immediately. This allows ample room to re-continue with the series with no disruptions.

In the Liabilities series, both current and non-current liabilities are placed in the "3000" series, with current liabilities range from "3000 to 3499" while the non-current range is from "3500 to 3999" series. There won't be that many liabilities in most cases, but for instance, in the banking sector, most of the money the bank holds for its customers is a liability. Couple this to interest income for customers and other benefits, making a big part of the liabilities. For them, a more extensive series sequence would be needed to accommodate the liability headings.

As explained, it all depends on your requirements regarding how you are willing to set the accounts out as these are the market practices, not regulatory requirements.

3. Owner's Equity and Equity Accounts

Owner's Equity sometimes takes a large share as it can include share capital, preference capital, reserved earnings, general earnings, etc. This series can start right after liabilities, which means in the "4000" series. Owner's equity can have variable account types in it, but it mostly covers the entire "4000" series to stay on the safer side of the functioning framework.

4. Revenue/ Income

As we advance, the series moves to revenue or income. You must remember that the revenue or income series is the business's primary revenue or income earned as part of its main operational activities. This revenue series is followed and allotted the "5000" series.

Revenue and income can be of many other types as well. For instance, it can also relate to other income earned, not as part of the main operational activity but as a side or secondary income source. This type of income is recorded under the "7000" series as it differs from primary revenue.

5. Expense/ Cost of Revenue or Sales

Assigning numbers to the accounts in the chart is easy, but the series must differentiate them to address those accounts properly. Expenses can be classified into different types. For instance, Expenses can be Costs of Sales/Revenue, Administrative expenses, Selling and Distribution expenses, or even the Finance Cost Expense. It is essential that each heading is separately identified and given a sequence too.

The series sequence that immediately follows the primary revenue is the Cost of Revenue or Cost of sales, given the series number of "6000 to 6800". This series has to be continued directly after the revenue series as it allows easy identification in the chart of accounts and the financial statements.

Other expenses such as administrative, selling and distribution, and marketing are categorized totally in the "7000" series. This can vary from range to range as some standard practices have a series gap of 300 or 250 before the other expense is started, and most practices just categorize the entire expense in these heads.

Make Your Decision Based on the Chart of Accounts

Regardless of how standard practices are followed, you must remember that you have full control and decision in making your own set of accounts. The real reason a standard technique should be followed is because of the consistency and similarity that allows another person to understand it easily. For example, if your business expands in the upcoming future or in the coming times, you might need to hire an accountant. That accountant must find it easy to understand the framework and the business model to adapt to the work environment and the working criteria. Common practice creates an elaborate but easy understanding of the fundamentals.

The numbering in the series doesn't matter because you can decide the number series at your own will, but the element flow should be followed in the aspects defined above. In software where the number indexing is still followed, these techniques will help a lot.

In QuickBooks Online, Xero, and other software, the number indexing is already pre-defined in the system. We are just responsible for creating the category names from our financial framework. Most software's Chart of Accounts can be navigated from the list option displayed in the upper menu bars or displayed in the company option in the upper menu bars.

Key Fundamentals to Make Sure of Consistency and Flexibility

From going through the process of setting up the Chart of Accounts, you may find that navigating the options is easy. There are things you should remember to make sure of consistency and flexibility.

- Make sure that you can adequately navigate your way around the option on your digital accounting software.

- It is an excellent approach to first draft out a rough format of the entire business model to understand your business model's quantifiable aspects. This will not only save time but also allow you to understand your framework.

- Don't forget to check out the pre-designed formats or sample company accounts present in the digital accounting software, as they will allow you to save time and edit only those aspects you require.

- During the setup process, remove account titles that don't relate to your business model. If your business is a service industry and supplies no goods, then having an account named inventory or stock in trade serves you no purpose.

- Keep things simple and easy to navigate. People can create a complicated chart of accounts that serves no purpose. So always keep everything simple and manageable and only to the extent of your needs.

- If your business model has future diversification expectations, avoid adding accounts that are not followed at earlier stages. Ensure that you only add those accounts you need and show your framework and financials appropriately as too much information or too much of the wrong effort can sometimes result in losing out on valuable resources.

• A wise decision is always to create many series so new heads of accounts can be added later on when the time comes. Give flexibility to your entire process so any change can be easily accounted for and doesn't cause a waste of resources.

Chapter 6: Transactions, Ledgers, and Journals

This section of the book will be more descriptive and provide accounting information and knowledge you need to understand these concepts:

- What is a transaction - and if non-financial transactions matter to your accounts

- What journals are - and their various types

- The ledger accounts and how they are used in digital accounting software

- How digital accounting software processes each phase and part of the accounting cycle

- Ideas on mastering the ledger and journal knowledge.

Now let's get started.

Are There Other Types of Transactions?

In the book's previous chapters, we have discussed the financial transactions and gave a little insight into non-financial transactions. By now, you may have understood what a transaction is and, if you look at your business, you may spot a few things that are not quantifiable. Yet, they do directly affect your business operations.

For instance, you have heard that a new law or a new regulation came up, preventing certain operational activities. This new regulation or law can't be quantified in terms of your business, but this regulation's impact directly interferes with your operations. You may ask yourself if this is even a transaction, and if you should account for it. The answer is "Yes" because this impacts your business and its operations. But what type of transaction is it?

These transactions are known as non-financial transactions, which may need to be accounted for similarly to any other financial transaction. This type of transaction is mostly disclosed, but it is sometimes adjusted in our accounts. These are all advanced concepts, and you need not get into that.

Whether financial or non-financial, the transactions are always considered part of the financial statements. And a transaction is an event that occurred in the past and affects the operations.

Journals and Ledgers: What are They?

For starters, Journal is commonly a short form for the Journal Book, which records and maintains all the transactions occurring in a day or a sequence, the latter of which may be chronological. And any record written in it is known as a Journal Entry.

Journals are the most basic and common forms of record maintaining. In small businesses, people have a book where they record every transaction which occurred in a day – this is the Journal Book. Journal Books are used for cash records and to maintain all the cash-related activities such as making a sale or purchasing an item. Each Journal Book represents a particular account for which the record is entered and maintained. This is known as a ledger.

A ledger is the representation of a particular account that shows the entire movement in it. Journal and Ledger are almost the same because a Journal Book has different types, such as Sales Day Book, Purchase Day Book, General Journal, and Petty Cash Book.

All these represent a particular type of account, and these particular accounts are considered ledgers. Journal and Ledgers are the same, but the difference is some journals only record one side of the transaction of an accounting system in it, either as a debit or a credit side transaction. Ledgers record *both sides.*

Start with Journal Types

As a small business owner, you may already have a system where you record all your financial transactions. This could include books where you recorded your sales, purchases, and other cash transactions, with each book serving a specific purpose.

The same concept follows here that the Journal Book has these types:

i.   Sales Day Book
ii.   Purchase Day Book
iii.   Cash Book
iv.   Petty Cash Book
v.   General Journal
vi.   Purchase Return Book
vii.   Sales Return Book

All these books have specified purposes; let's take a look at each.

1. Sales Day Book

The Sales Day Book records all the credit transactions that occur when selling goods or services to the customer. These books record all the sales made on credit that occurred in the entire day and then create a total amount of the credit sales made to the customers. These books have a standard four columns in which serial number, description, invoice number, and the total amount are recorded. These books can also be customized according to your needs.

2. Purchase Day Book

Unlike the Sales Day Book, the Purchase Day Book records credit type transactions on purchasing goods or services. The total purchases that occurred in the day are recorded here and kept in chronological order. With the same standard format of four columns, purchase day books easily allow the entrepreneurs to keep track of their liabilities.

3. Cash Book

The Cash Book is the prime basis of the ledger formations. The cash book records all the cash transactions that occurred during the entire day or specific period. The Cash Book has both sides of the common T-ledger accounts: a debit side and a credit side. It is recorded on the cash book's left side whenever cash is received, meaning its debit side. It is recorded on the credit or right side of the Cash Book whenever cash is spent.

The Cash Book became the first-ever foundation to the ledger accounts as both sides of a ledger account has a debit and a credit balance to balance out the accounting equation. There is one major loophole in the cash book: when an asset is purchased, it is considered an expense, and it is written on the credit side of the cash book. And when loans or other financing are taken from the bank or any other financial institution, it is a liability recorded on the debit side as cash received. Accountants are careful when examining the cash book because they are looking for various assets and liabilities.

The Cash Book commonly has a two-column type that records the cash at hand and cash at bank transaction, but sometimes the petty cash is also recorded in the Cash Book, which then becomes a three-column type Cash Book. These columns are defined by the various other cash accounts being recorded in the same Cash Book.

4. Petty Cash Book

The Petty Cash Book is the same as a Sales Day Book or Purchase Day Book. It records all the petty expenses which were incurred during the day. Sometimes the petty cash Book is merged with the same central Cash Book and is called a three-column Cash Book.

5. General Ledger

The general ledger records all such transactions that didn't involve cash and excludes all sales and purchases. When the term "sales" or "purchases" is used, it refers to the common sales and purchases made in the current business practice., which can be different depending upon the industry. For instance, a watch-making industry would record sales of watches and purchases of the dials and the glass frame.

The general ledger acts as the dual entry accounting system where it records a debit and a credit, as mentioned before in the previous chapters. Examples of the transactions recorded in this book include credit purchase of a vehicle, depreciation charged on the assets or bad debts, etc.

6. Sales Return Day Book

This book records all the customer sales returns and typically those to whom credit sales were made. The cash sales return is recorded in the cash book, but the credit sales return is recorded in the sales return day Book.

7. Purchase Return Day Book

The Purchase Return Day Book is the same, just like the Sales Return Day Book, Sales Day Book, and Purchase Day Book, but it maintains the suppliers' purchase returns records. It only records credit purchase returns made in a day as the cash purchase returns are recorded in the Cash Book. It also has four columns in total that are the same in the Sale Day Book or the Purchase Day Book.

All these Journal Entry Books are also known as the Books of Prime Entry. This is because these books record and maintain all the financial records at the initial stage of the accounting cycle, the recording phase.

Being an entrepreneur, you may need to use these books as well because they have various advantages.

- These books help keep the entire record in physical form in chronological order
- All records maintained in these books are based on receipts or bills
- These help in accounting for all events that occur daily and as part of the reconciliation processes
- Whenever the auditor requires the details of the transactions, they can also find them in the records present in these books

What Differentiates a Journal from a Ledger?

A ledger is one element of an account containing debits and credits. The real concept of ledgers came into effect from the cash book which small business owners used to maintain.

In a cash book, the left side represents how much money is received and when. Thus, when an asset increases, it is represented as a debit. Similarly, the cash book's right side represents all the cash payments made during the entire period, represented as a credit because it is credited when an asset decreases. This is how the common T-ledger concept came into effect.

To illustrate what a T ledger is, please have a look at the image.

Debit			Bank A/c	Credit	
Date	Particulars	Amount	Date	Particulars	Amount
Jun-19	To sales	80,000	Feb-19	By purchases	45,000
Sep-19	To accounts receivable	30,000	Aug-19	By rent	12,000
			Oct-19	By other expenses	22,000
				By balance carried to balance sheet	
			Dec-19	(balancing figure)	31,000
	Total	1,10,000		Total	1,10,000

The T-ledger has a left side, the debit side, and the right side, the credit side. Now a T-ledger represents one single account. For instance, it can represent a cash account, a vehicle account, a bank loan account, etc. This makes it completely different from the journal because some journals accommodate a single effect, either as a debit or credit.

What Purpose Does the Ledger Serve?

Ledgers are the final entry books that show the dual entry accounting system. It is the start point when all information is appropriately classified and recorded in its relevant headings. Each ledger heading describes separate categories of the account. To prepare financial statements, each heading's closing balance is used after a certain period.

Ledger balances such as income and expenses have to be grouped in the profit-and-loss statement, and they have no opening balance. Ledger headings such as assets, liabilities, and owner's equity do close, but their opening balances always exist in the next period. Being an entrepreneur, you have to extra careful to make sure that every relevant ledger heading is correctly classified into the accounting element. Otherwise, your accounts would be mismanaged and improperly disclosed.

The ledger serves variable other functions such as:

- It ensures that all relevant transactions are accounted for in their appropriate headings.
- It detects any errors, which may arise in calculating the closing balances of each ledger's headings.
- It maintains consistency in preparing reports and other such documents in the later stages when all accounts are closed for the period.

Post Entries on the Ledger

Entrepreneurs must learn every single aspect of their business. Sometimes, you may also spend hours trying to understand an insignificant point and trying to work out the answer. While trying to understand your business's financial aspects, you may feel confused or worried, especially when you understand the dual entry system.

How is a double entry formed?

Go over this section as often as you need to, ensuring you understand it thoroughly. Posting in Ledgers means that when the double entry of a transaction is made, it is recorded in the heading where it belongs. The confusion at this stage is because:

a. You may create or pass a wrong double entry, which will corrupt the information.

b. You may pass the double entry correctly but post it on the wrong side of the ledgers.

To mitigate the first error, the double entries will be explained below.

Debit		Credit
Assets	=	Liabilities
Expenses		Income
Drawings		Capital

This concept was explained earlier. Naturally, some account elements are found on the debit side, while some are found on the credit side. While performing double entry, you must remember how transactions would represent each element of the account.

For instance,

I. Expenses Dr.- When we incur expenses or when expenses increase, it is debited.

- If the payment made is through cash, then Cash at hand or cash at the bank would be credited. The reason is that when we pay an expense, our cash gets reduced. When an asset decreases, it is credited.

a. Cash in Hand/Cash at Bank A/C Cr.

- If the payment isn't made through cash and instead, we incurred the expense but have not paid, it means we must pay later on. It is the company's/business's liability. Here, when a liability increases, it is naturally credited.

b. Liability/Trade Payable A/C Cr.

Similarly,

II. Income Cr. – When we sell goods or provide services, we earn income, and when income increases, it is naturally credited.

- If the business received the money instantly for performing the services, then our asset, i.e., cash, will increase, and when an asset increases, it is debited.

a. Cash in hand/Cash at Bank A/C Dr.

- Suppose the customer receives the business's services and doesn't pay the money right away, saying he will pay later. There, it means that the money is due by that person and is the business's receivable. Thus, receivable is an asset on which we have the right, and when an asset increases, it is debited.

b. Receivables/Trade Debtor Dr.

From these explanations, one thing is clear: when certain accounts increase, they naturally show how they correspond, i.e., debit if an asset, expense of drawing is increased, and credit if income, liability, or capital increases. Remember that you can differentiate an asset, expense, liability, income, and capital when accounting and posting transactions by a double-entry system. Otherwise, the common mistake will continue resulting in inaccurate accounts.

The explanation presented eradicates only one confusion. The other confusion, which still exists, is posting the ledger's transactions. For this, always remember that when you pass the correct journal entry, just place the accounts' values on the same side with the other entry's corresponding name.

For instance,

I. Expense Dr.

- When you pass the entry, you must place the value of the expense on the T-ledger's debit side but must use the account's corresponding name that caused the expense to be debited.

a. If the expense was paid in the form of cash, you must use the name of cash on the expense ledger's debit side.

b. If the expense was not paid and accrued, you must use the name of liability on the debit side of the expense ledger.

II. **Income Cr.**

- When you pass the entry, you must place the value of the income on the T-ledger's credit side, but you must use the corresponding name which caused the account to be credited.

a. If the income was credited because of the customer's cash, then the name of cash will be used on the income ledger's credit side. Similarly, the debit side will represent income as the debit side's narration in the cash ledger.

b. If the income was credited, but the customer agreed to pay on a later date, then, in this case, the income ledger will represent the name or receivable on its credit side. Simultaneously, the receivables ledger will be debited with the name of income on its debit side.

These narrations often play a crucial when reconciling the items or tracing transactions in the entire system.

How Digital Accounting Made Posting Easy

Many of you might still feel confused about the entire accounting system. Luckily, digital accounting software made it easy for everyone to use with minimum confusion.

When you provide a service, this digital software generates the invoice on its own once you complete the data. Then it automatically passes the double entry in both of the relevant accounts. The income is credited in the Chart of Accounts, and the other account, cash or receivable, is also debited.

This software has advanced so much that each aspect of the business is automatically handled using the double-entry system. Whether you are buying an asset, receiving funds, or even making an expense, all the work is done automatically, making the work streamlined.

Digital Accounting: Accounting Each Phase

The previous chapter explained what type of digital accounting would serve best for your needs. Now we will detail how this software will guarantee that every procedure runs and performs accurately.

The accounting cycle is far more complicated when it has to be evaluated by the professional accountants on how systems can adapt and respond appropriately. As an entrepreneur, the evaluation doesn't concern you, but these systems' useful functionality does.

The journalism and the ledger formation can become tricky when it is handled manually. Their use can sometimes lead to unknown consequences and errors, which can become complicated and nearly impossible for you to handle. The accounting cycle revolves around the concept of how transactions can be recorded, summarized, and reported, but the far broader aspect of it always starts after reporting.

For most small business owners, the trick isn't to develop a accommodated system that supports your business but enhances your working criteria to make sure things go smoothly and securely. From recording to reporting, everything is easily managed on digital software.

Automatic Transaction Recording and Posting

When you look into the digital systems' recording portion, you will see that from invoicing, managing the cost of sales, asset management tabs to even debt scheduling, etc., everything is present.

I. Revenue

The invoicing system present in each digital software automatically passes the double-entry once we make the invoice. Whether the transaction is cash or credit, the system takes care of the double entry. Not only that, but the track downs would also allow you to trace the payments and when made. Once payments are made, the system only asks for the amount and invoice against which the payment was received. Afterward, the system automatically books the double-entry by reducing the receivable and increasing the cash in the account.

II. Cost of Sales and Expenses

The systems also incorporate all the bills received from the suppliers, whether they are cash or credit. Once the bill is recorded in the system, the double entry is done automatically, including payment of the supplier's invoices.

III. Assets

Most popular digital systems like QuickBooks have an asset management program that records all the assets and passes their double-entry system on their own once purchased on cash. For an asset's credit purchase, the general entry would have to be passed manually.

IV. Liabilities

The common liabilities of trade creditors, i.e., suppliers, are recorded in expenses, but bank loans are not included. This can also be incorporated into double entry automatically. This can be done from the banking tabs present in the digital systems.

Automatic Summarization and Reporting Transactions

Since the system automatically performs all the recording and posting work of the transactions, it can easily summarize all the ledgers and prepare the trial balance. Not only that, but it can also produce various reports for every user's needs.

Chapter 7: Processing Payroll and Taxes

This chapter will go over the essential ideas and concepts regarding business taxes and employee taxes. Let's get started.

What is Business Tax and Is It Different?

You may already know fully what tax is and why tax is paid., but the actual question on your mind wouldn't be what benefits tax has, but rather how your business manages its taxes and stays aware of the ever-changing laws.

You must remember the first essential rule in the business world: the owner and the business are two separate entities. The reason is that the Companies Law or Ordinance (depending on your business function) demands that both, i.e., you and your business, be considered two different entities. In law, the terminology used for "person" includes businesses and companies considered artificial persons.

This is done to evaluate taxes on different bases. Most individuals pay different amounts of taxes to their respective authorities because every person has different income sources that fall under different tax calculation rates. The same case applies to businesses. According to their business model, many businesses have different tax rates and tax amounts, which helps everyone evaluate appropriately.

Thus, business taxes differ from regular taxes that a person pays, and this type of tax is levied on your business's single or various sources of income.

How to Manage Various Types of Taxes

The two major types of taxes, which your business must handle will include:

- Tax-related to Business operations
- Tax-related specifically to payrolls

There are other forms of taxes, but only these two types of taxes shall be mentioned to keep ideas and topics consistent and straightforward

1. Tax-Related to Business Operations

Tax-related to business operations technically involves all the taxes directly or indirectly levied upon the business itself. This doesn't mean it will only include the income tax. Income tax is levied upon the turnover and net profits before taxation, but there are other forms of taxes such as:

I. **Property Tax** – Tax levied upon the commercial building if owned.

II. **Sales Tax** – Tax levied upon the sale of goods or services.

III. **Value Added Tax** - Tax levied upon the goods or merchandise to increase its cost.

Property tax will be charged if you own any commercial building, and the business itself must pay this tax if the business has the property under its name. For instance, in the US, the S-Corp, i.e., Small Business Corporation, is a separate legal entity and can own real estate and other assets. The Sales tax is levied upon the provincial, state, or even federal government's orders on the sale of goods and services. Sales tax typically varies a lot depending upon the customer as different rates apply in different regions. For instance, in India, there are different sales tax rates for some states.

While managing your operations as a businessman, you would have to manage these taxes. They are different taxes, and the consequences of each are different in the eyes of the law. Many people consider that income tax is the only tax they are responsible for paying. However, these taxes must also be managed when taking income tax into the business's growth perspective.

2. Tax-Related Specifically to Payroll

Payroll taxes are a completely different variable. They are related to the payroll taxes, which the business has to withhold from the employees' payroll when making the salary payment or paid by your business if the contract states that the employer will pay all taxes. These mostly include:

    I.Social Security and Medicare Taxes
    II.Federal Income tax withholding on Salaries
    III.Federal Unemployment tax

These taxes are sometimes paid by the employer, which is you in this case, while other times, these taxes are paid by the employees, and it is withheld from their salary payments.

The employee's salary typically plays an essential part in the business because you would have to calculate the amount of tax every month of each employee before paying them. And this will be especially needed if you have three or more employees as this can become a burden if left unmanaged.

Your business needs to keep up with the new employee benefits and payroll taxes as they are ever-changing. The primary responsibility of tax collection from employees or individuals lies with the business because it provides ease in the government's work.

Nowadays, managing business taxes and employee payroll taxes can be tricky when running all its significant aspects. However, many businesses have been able to keep up and maintain their business and taxes through digital systems. Digital systems like QuickBooks, Xero, and others have made things easy, opening doors to vast new opportunities that entrepreneurs can explore.

Processing Payroll on Your Own

Your goal is just like any other businessman's goal: lowering costs to increase profits. Processing your payroll is one way to accomplish this. There are many types of payroll software to make this job easier, so you can sit back and relax.

1. Set Up the Payroll Functionality Manually

Setting up the payroll manually can be a time-consuming task. Still, if you believe that your business model won't integrate with the pre-defined payroll functionality, you can have the payroll features setup as per your needs. Since most digital software has an open feature to allow manual setups and manual edits, you will find using them beyond satisfactory.

I. Select the Payroll Software

For more information about payroll software is the best (and which should be avoided), please refer to chapter 4: 10 Tools for Digital Accounting. That chapter elaborates on requirements that best suit your business model.

However, when selecting the payroll software, you must remember whether you want a centralized digital system or a decentralized system. The payroll service providing software rarely is centralized and differs entirely from the main accounting software. Thus, it is essential that when selecting a payroll software, you select that software best for you and saves you time.

II. Add Your Employee List

The second step in payroll tax processing is to make sure your employee list has complete details with complete documentation. Before you can even create a payroll, you need to have employees introduced to pay the salaries. Details regarding employees can include name, address, social security number, employee identification number, the national identity card number (SS# in the US), working hours, salary, etc.

Suppose you are uploading the information for the first time. There, you will face no issue other than the time consumption factor, but if you already have a payroll service available and are looking to shift, this will cause serious problems as you would have to add all the data employees all over again.

III. Set the Payroll Tax Parameters

Once you have completed all the documents and input the employee list, the next step is to navigate the employee payroll section to create a manual setup. In this setup, you will find various tabs asking you for various information regarding the employees, work, and yourself.

Afterward, you must create the manual tax deduction and allowance charts to perform an automatic process. After this, you will need to ensure that the account's relevant heading is mentioned where the payroll tax liabilities will be credited. For instance, if the payment has to be made to the Federal government under the Federal Unemployment Tax Act (US), you need to mention the authority's name that will receive the tax.

Similarly, once this is done, you must enter the new rates and other tax rates applicable to the employee's payroll.

IV. Organize the Due Dates

This step involves setting up the dates for each payment type, which will be made based on your business. These dates include salary payments, tax payments, and other such payments, etc. You must know and understand the dates on which you must make various payments.

V. Track Time and Record It

Once everything is set up, then it is time to put your operations into motion. Input or allow automatic time tracking software to track the working hours of the employees. This way, you won't even have to enter the time or punch the time in the timesheets manually.

You could also manually enter the time, but that will be time-consuming. Many payroll software and even accounting software offer the automatic time tracking feature and records the time worked in the weekly timesheets and simply wait for your approval.

VI. Automatic Tax Calculations

If you selected the most popular accounting software on the market, you're in luck. QuickBooks will perform automatic tax calculations on your payroll and simply report the amount you must pay your employees. QuickBooks helps you focus more on your business.

But suppose you selected software that doesn't automatically calculate payroll. There, you must spend additional time each month to calculate payable salary to employees. Much online software doesn't even offer automatic tax calculations, which make your day-to-day tasks challenging and frustrating.

Not only that, but the automatic tax calculation software will also withhold the income tax payable by the employees to the federal government.

VII. Pay the Taxes and File Your Business Returns

If you have software that calculates all the taxes payable by your employees and tax payable by your business (on income), you'll have an easier time during tax season – all year round! If you keep updated software (rules and regulations), the program will complete such entries within moments; you only check for the correct amount payable (which the software will provide if timesheets or salary is entered), and you are finished!

Many software products have manual payroll, and, as such, you'll have to perform those tricky calculations yourself – every pay period. Choose your payroll software (or entire software package carefully, ensuring that automatic functions cover all the calculations, not just a few.

2. Outsource Your Payroll

The smartest approach, which many business owners and accountants use, is outsourcing payroll. Different areas of a business, including the support departments such as IT services, HR Department, and bookkeeping, can be easily outsourced while managing your costs. The perfect balance between time, resources, and costs is always achievable by outsourcing the work.

Whether you are just starting your business or running your operations for some time, payroll service providers will get your job done – a real timesaver.

Choose Your Service Provider

When you choose your service provider, consider these three things:

- How much is it going to save you?
- How efficiently will the task be managed?
- How good is their customer service?

I. Upload Your Employee List

Before setting up your employee list with the service provider, you need to ensure that all the documents and related information regarding the employees are complete. If you are using the service providing software for the first time, you will find uploading the information and documents relatively easy and quick.

However, if you switch from your current package to a new package, you must go through the process again. When selecting a payroll service, choose carefully; otherwise, you may end paying considerably more rather than saving a few bucks.

II. Tracking Time and Hours Worked

Many software products support a single device or a single computer that uploads time and tracks hours worked; this keeps other employees from uploading their time on other systems. However, some newer and improved software versions automatically track and import time from the employees' work environment interface. These automatically detect and track time, allowing employees to focus on their work while the software notes every activity from the background.

You may find this software more beneficial because it detects and records every activity. You simply approve or reject the time tracked on the systems.

Once all the time has been uploaded and recorded, you can import all the data at each month's end to reconcile with the number of hours each employee worked.

III. Processing the Payments and Taxes

The final step is automatic, where the service provider keeps track of every single liability and processes the payroll payment for the employees. Besides this, they also process the tax payments for the relevant authorities.

A Key Point When Processing Payroll and Taxes

A few crucial points and critical tips for avoiding untoward consequences include:

• Many people rely heavily on software, and reliance on technology is good, but you need to be mindful of what you input when tracking and auditing your system.

• You need an accountant to perform an audit sometimes regarding the system's operation because this will help you see the more accurate picture.

• Remember to select a trusted software product with fantastic reviews for customer service; you'll need a responsive resource if something goes wrong!

- Your system functions just like your business; it will demand time to learn and implement, so expect that.

- Remember to keep a physical record of every single payroll processed and reconcile it regularly with the system so you can spot any discrepancies.

- Always remember to have a check and balance procedure in place to avoid major mishaps.

- Ensure all the documentation regarding payroll is available early because taxes must be paid.

- You need to keep up with the ever-changing laws and consult an accountant when you feel unclear about the law.

- Remember to check all the business taxes, which apply to your business income sources. Sometimes, new forms of taxes can be levied by the government, so ensure that you are well informed.

As an entrepreneur, you may find that your business's core areas can be managed independently. Still, you need to know that a consultant from an accountant is there to help whenever you face any issue (or anything that seems unclear).

Other forms of taxes need to be managed from time after time, but you might never have to face these as a small-medium owner. Ensure that your business is also registered with the relevant government entities - check state and local laws.

Chapter 8: Financial Statements

Let's look at the importance of financial statements, including an in-depth explanation of income statements, balance sheets, cash flow statements, and owner's equity.

Financial Statements: What are they?

When you run your own business, you want to know how it is performing at any given time, and you can assess this by looking at your business profits or losses. When a business is said to be healthy, that tends to refer to the number of customers or average sales per day.

Financial statements are the summarized form of the entire business affairs and performance for a particular period. They are those reports that allow you and other third parties to assess your business. For most business owners, financial statements are the ultimate objective of understanding how the business operates in a year.

To assess business performance, typically, the prime indicator is the profit or loss statement, which is now called "Statement of Comprehensive Income." This statement is primarily the document that concerns you and your business partners and investors. However, the profit and loss statement only defines its revenues and how it manages its assets and other liabilities. For this, other statements are in place to solve the concerns which many investors have.

Financial statements are the most important business document for any company because almost everyone relies on these reports and uses them to make business decisions. If you apply for a loan, the commercial banks will ask you for the financial statements before considering your application, as will any other credit company you apply to.

Start with an Income Statement

Every business earns income and has expenses and, each year, these are tracked in the financial accounts to allow for accurate reporting. The profit and loss statement (or income statement) consists of the following account headings:

- **Revenue** - this is the principal activity of the business for which the company earns income
- **Cost of Sales or Cost of Revenue** - considered the costs incurred to earn the business's principal activity's revenues
- **Gross Profit** - Calculated when we subtract the cost of revenues or sales from the primary revenues. Gross profit margin plays an essential role in assessing whether the company's operations are earning or losing money on each sale. If the gross profit margins are negative, meaning the company is losing on every sale of goods or service, it means that the company may soon shut down its operations.
- **Administrative Expenses** - Admin expenses mostly include the expenses, which indirectly relate to the operations. These expenses include the office, accounts department, IT department, HR department, and other office expenses. These are categorized separately in the profit and loss statement under the other operating expenses.

- **Selling and Distribution Expenses** - selling and distribution expenses include all those relating to delivering goods to the customer or any commissions related to the sale. This is mostly found in the manufacturing industry, where the goods are distributed to regional branches and sold.

- **Marketing and Advertising Expenses** – Operating expenses, marketing, and advertising expenses include advertising, promotion, and sales commission. Along with that, it also includes the salaries of the marketing and advertising department.

- **Finance Cost** - Finance cost includes all the financial charges and expenses based on paying interest or charges to the bank. This is categorized under *non-operating* expenses.

- **Net Profit** - Net profit is the final stage of the profit calculation, where all the expenses are subtracted from the gross profit. Net profit depicts whether the business can earn a profit after all the indirect expenses related to it. For a business to grow, it is crucial to know whether the business can sustain its operations or grow its operations further, which is determined by this figure.

There are two types of net profit, one is before taxation, and the other is after taxation. The Statement of Comprehensive Income also includes unrealized gains belonging in Other Comprehensive Income, but this is an advanced concept. Before taxation, the net profit gives a partial idea of whether the business can sustain its current economic model.

The taxation expense plays a heavily crucial role as it shows whether the government supports the business function. If the business faces high market instability and higher taxes, the net profit after tax will be heavily disrupted. It will show that no matter how much revenue the business makes, it can never expand while in the current region or country.

This financial analysis, how to read financial statements, and each account heading will be explained in the next chapter. For now, you must remember how the income statement is made.

If you opted to use digital accounting software, the financial statements could be generated instantly with a click of a button; we'll discuss this later.

Balancing the Equation: The Balance Sheet

In the previous chapter, we explained the accounting equation. You may have seen that the accounting equation is always balanced due to the double-entry system, showing an accurate picture of the company's affairs.

For instance, if you are concerned about your business, you will not rely on your business's profit and loss statement, as it doesn't show an accurate picture of your business's strength and value. Thus, you need a statement that shows how many assets your business has to contribute more to the investing activities. Along with that, you also need to check how many liabilities and debts your company has and whether financing options are available.

Similarly, the balance sheet or financial position statement elaborates on the accounting equation and summarizes it into a report.

Thus, the balance sheet or financial position statement gives a more detailed view of the company's affairs. Much of the information regarding assets, liabilities, and owner's equity has been given in previous chapters. Please refer to them to clarify anything you do not understand.

Statement of Cashflow

The statement of cash flows reflects the cash ledger in report format. If the cash method is used for accounting, cash flow would be the entire profit and loss statement along with the balance sheet. If the accrual method were followed for accounting, you would need to create the cash flow statement as third parties will not access your accounts.

Thus, the cash flow statement shows the cash earned and cash spent. The cash flow statement is presented in two forms:

> I. Direct method- Where the cash ledger is presented in report form.
>
> II. Indirect method- The statement of profit and loss and Balance sheet is used to report the cash flows.

The IFRS and GAAP promote the use of the indirect method for presenting the statement of cash flow because it sub-divides the entire cash flow into three parts:

- Cash flow from operations
- Cash flow from investing activities
- Cash flow from financing activities

These three parts of the cash flow statements give a more vivid picture of the business's cash flow and show whether the operational activities earn money.

Statement of Changes in Owner's Equity

The statement of changes in owner's equity gives the information regarding the opening equity, the profit and loss for the year, any dividends or drawings made, and the closing equity. The statement of changes also shows the information regarding the owners' capital in the business.

How Digital Accounting Tools Generate These Reports

Even though an accountant is required for an in-depth understanding of these reports, you can get by with a basic understanding of them.

Typically, every accounting software has a built-in report function where the reports are automatically generated. Here, your job would be only to enter the range and the data to extract from the reports. Once you press ok, all the reports will be presented, and almost every single accounting software has accessibility to the general reporting functionalities.

You can also edit these reports manually if you feel heads of accounts are wrongly reported. Simply by downloading the entire report to an excel sheet, you can easily extract and then edit these reports. Note that not all accounting software has these functionalities, but most of these extractions of reports and other downloading features are found in the reports or reporting section.

Some of these digital tools extract reports in other ways as well. Some of them give direct access to various other reports. For instance, if you access the revenue by customer report (if such a report is present in your package), you will automatically access the payment tracks made by the customer. One of the best features of digital tools is that other than principal financial statements preparation, they also facilitate making other reports. For service industries, reports could be like profit and loss per client project, unbilled hours per client, pending reimbursable allowances and expenses, revenue per customer, etc. all these reports allow a great analysis of reports, which will be explained in the next chapter.

Tips to Remember When You Generate Financial Statements

Some general tips regarding the financial statements are:

- Generate financial statements and record entries each month to keep the information intact and secure.
- Financial statements can be easily prepared, but don't give these statements to third-parties without consulting your accountant, as relevant disclosures and other information may be missing from these statements.

- Remember to make sure that your financial statements are the key basis of documents used *in every place*. Don't prepare different sets to submit in different places. This will make information inconsistent and result in fraudulent activities.

- Remember to have a reconciliation check and an estimation check when you are finished preparing the financial statements. This will allow you to see whether the figures reported are accurate.

Even though you and many people try their best to keep information consistent, sometimes, things get out of hand due to time pressure and other issues. So always remember to give proper time to your financial information to keep work undisrupted.

Chapter 9: Analyzing Financial Statements

This chapter will focus entirely on reading the financial statements and how they interpret the information present.

From recording your business transaction events to concluding it on the financial statements, you and everyone associated with your business now just have one concern - how the business performed compared to the previous years and what it means for its future outlook. You might think that your business is at the top right now, but every recorded transaction paints a picture of the previous year. Those who are concerned about the business will estimate and decide the future outlook of the business.

Every transaction you have recorded regarding your business was related to past events. These events have already occurred and been recorded, but potential investors, current investors, and any official body that needs to assess ongoing performance need to understand how the business will grow in the future. For this, top-level investors use multiple techniques, seeking valuable input from your business's performance history, creating a whole scenario in terms of their decision-making.

Can Financial Analysis Give Predictions About Business Performance?

In the stock market, the most prominent trading activities occur over the day, and investors do all these trading activities. From small to medium to even large investors, these investors continuously monitor and observe the stock market patterns and their performance before deciding. These investors sometimes have an expert team of accountants and brokers who work in close coordination all the time. When a deal is ready to be struck, these investors take the chances. However, they assume the companies' working performance and then estimate when they will close their stock market positions.

The exact methods they use, the trends they observe, and the timings all matter to them, and these techniques and methods they use are followed on the financial analysis concept. The financial analysis doesn't involve only checking and comparing figures; it also means estimating the business's trends and patterns.

From the stock market example, you can better understand financial analysis. Any person with basic know-how regarding accounts will also use some of these basic techniques to assess their performance.

Basic Overview: How Financial Analysis is Done

The profit and loss statement shows these elements: revenue, the cost of sales or cost of revenue, the gross profit, operating profit, profit before tax, and profit after tax. Before you even consider the financial analysis techniques, the P&L should be considered. For instance, the moment you receive the profit and loss statement of your business, you can see, at a glance, what is happening and the potential prospects.

Profit and loss isn't the only thing that defines your business growth. For instance, the real reason behind loss or low profits this year might be higher interest and finance costs. Now it isn't safe to assume that your business won't perform properly or perform the same in the future. The best approach would be to cut out the cost by making more principal payments on the loans to reduce the finance cost. Financial analysis doesn't involve decision-making; it gives a rough comparison or idea regarding the business compared with the previous year.

But for now, let's move on ahead with basic financial analysis ideas and decision-making in some instances.

1. Revenue and Gross Profits

You already know what revenue is and how gross profit is calculated. Now let's imagine a situation - the revenue is $1,000,000 while the gross profit is $455,000. Automatically, you will figure out that the cost of revenue or cost of sales is $545,000, i.e., (Revenue – Cost of Revenue/ Sales = Gross Profit, Cost of Sales/ Revenue = Revenue – Gross profit). What you won't realize is the percentage that represents the total revenue. You might wonder why you would need even to find the percentage, and here's the reality: Many businesses have a fixed percentage change between their revenue and gross profits directly proportional and, which has a minor 1- 3% variation. For you, a gross profit of 45.5% of total revenue may seem like an achievement, but what if another business's just like yours earns 55% to 60% of their total revenue as gross profit? When we compare it like this, it clearly shows there are many or significant inefficiencies that may be causing a high cost of sales.

The reasons may include having more labor force and fewer machines, saving a heavy depreciation cost, or their working techniques could be more efficient than the ones you are using. Some of the common inefficiencies could be:

- Use of high-end equipment, which requires heavy maintenance. Maintenance is related to the revenue projects and is categorized in Cost of Sales or revenue, but it doesn't include significant inspection or replacement of parts as these are assets)

- Lack of labor or personnel. This can also include inefficient use of the labor force. (Labors and other workers who are directly involved in the manufacturing or service providing processes are also categorized in cost of sales)

- Purchase of expensive raw materials or incurring excessive overhead charges

This type of financial analysis allows you to make an industry-wide comparison to see how your business performs compared with different competitors.

Now the actual decision-making is left to you, whether you would change the processes or enhance them according to your business model to increase the gross profit margins. This type of decision solely relies on you, but you must account for every single aspect, such as losing profits, which you might suffer from a change in methods, losing personnel, the cost savings, which will be observed, etc.

2. Revenue, Gross Profit, and Net Profit Before Taxation

Continuing the same example mentioned above, let's say that the net profit before taxation is $200,000, whereas the gross profit was $455,000. If we further break the operating expenses down, we will see that the operating expenses, including administrative, marketing, and distribution expenses, cost $105,000. The non-operating expenses, which include finance costs, are only $150,000. Keeping this in mind, we can see that the operating expenses are only 10.5% of the total revenue of $1,000,000. This is promising for your business because most industry-wide operating expenses range from 10-15% of the total revenue. Whether you are a service or a manufacturing industry, operating expenses can't go much lower than this unless operations are small. However, the finance cost is 15% of the total revenue., which is bad because finance cost shouldn't exceed more than the operating expenses.

If we interpret all this information, you understand that the business's finance cost, i.e., that interest expenses shouldn't be that high. It means that the business is heavily financing itself to keep itself afloat. Not only that, if we see that last year's finance costs were less, it means the business took on new loans. Looking at the administrative expenses, since it represents only 10% of the gross revenue, it means that the business should focus on maintaining this ratio. However, if these costs represent over 20% of the total revenue, then the only way to reduce these costs is by increasing revenues or cut the costs.

It is your decision as to whether (and how) you can sustain the business. The best way to reduce the finance cost is by making larger principal repayments on the loans. Principal repayments on loans cause lower finance costs to be borne by the business. Or the alternative way to reduce the finance cost is by utilizing non-interest options such as investment in the business or business associate's formation. Your decision-making on operating expenses lies solely in cutting costs and increasing revenues in the short term.

3. Net Profit Before Taxation and Net Profit After Taxation

As the net profit before tax is $200,000 and net profit after tax is $120,000, you may realize that taxation also plays a significant role in the profits. From this perspective, taxation is only 8% of the total revenue, but the actual comparison of taxation is never made based on total revenue. It is made based on both net profits before and after tax. The taxation is usually charged on the net profits before taxation. If the tax is $80,000, that means it is 40% of the net profit before tax. This is not good; it means the government or the tax authorities aren't considering the business class. The business taxes shouldn't be over 20% to 25% of the net profit before tax.

Once you interpret this, you will realize that the business model needs to be where the taxes can be saved and costs to run the business are minimal. The government sometimes facilitates the business class by incentivizing them with various investment options. As an entrepreneur or a businessman, you need to look for places where your tax can be saved or reduced. When the business keeps more cash and profits, it incentivizes the business to work more and continue its operations. If that isn't the case, it forces businesses to run on debts or loans, causing even more significant business issues.

However, if we look at it from this perspective that the net profit after tax is 12% of the total revenue, it means that the business has excellent potential to grow in the future. But it also means that for every sale of $1, the business earns $.12 as profit.

Decision-making now lies again with you regarding the reduction of the taxes. Taxes can be reduced only if the business model is aligned with something that the tax authorities incentivize. Business incentives can help keep the business going and prosperous over a few years, making them beneficial to you as you will save more cash and more profits by running the business. Ultimately, this will provide larger returns, more cash, better profitability status, more loans for future operational growth, more significant investments, and higher asset turnover.

You can also take various tax credits that your business can receive from its operation or other miscellaneous activities. For this expert advice and other information, consult a tax consultant or an accountant as they will provide you with up-to-date techniques and ways for you to reduce your taxation expenses.

Financial Analysis: Compare it with the Previous Year

The typical financial analysis that managers and the upper management perform compares the previous years' financial results. Here, the previous years or year is the base year. Every aspect, such as revenue, cost of revenue, gross profit, operating expenses, etc., is compared with the new recent year results. For example, if you ever look at a listed company's financial statements, you will find the director's report to provide these fundamental analyses to their shareholders. The comparisons include the financial results of the previous five years.

You will also compare with the previous year to help you understand and find areas that have become ineffective this year. Usually, these are used to determine whether the costs have increased or decreased disproportionately with the revenue. The comparison with the previous year's provides other insights. For instance,

- The incremental costs are incurred when revenue increases after a certain point
- The cost of running operations to the cost of manufacturing the product or providing the services
- The taxation impact over the successive years

The Complex Analysis: Profit and Loss with Balance Sheet

Even though the balance sheet can be explained in this chapter's introductory overview section, a proper understanding can be achieved only with profit and loss. When these two statements work simultaneously, they reveal a whole new picture regarding the business's performance and future expected affairs.

We explained a few assumptions present regarding the balance sheet from the profit and loss statement. For instance, we explained that the cost of raw materials might have become expensive, increasing sales costs. This also means that our inventory (which is the current asset) will also be higher than the previous year. Another example of this is when we mentioned that the finance cost increased in this year. The main reason could be that either fresh borrowings were taken this year or the interest rates drastically increased. This is related to current and non-current liabilities that non-current bank loans (which won't be payable within the next twelve months) have increased. Or that the current liabilities (which will be payable within the next twelve months) have a drastic increase in their amount, which is interest expense accrued.

Thus, we have shown a few examples of how profit and loss correlate to the balance sheet when seen together. Comparing the balance sheet with the previous year can be helpful. Still, this comparison is almost 90% covered in the cash flow statements, which show all the actual amount of increase or decrease. The comparison we are trying to interpret out of both statements relates to operational decision-making.

1. The Current Ratio and Quick Ratio: Cash Flow Recovery

The key elements, which will be interlinked in the current ratio, will include revenue, cost of sales, accounts receivables, inventory, advances, trade creditors, and other payables. The current ratio is essentially the current assets divided by the current liabilities, showing how much cash will be received and how much cash will be paid in the short run. The essential ratio the current assets and current liabilities should maintain is 2: 1. That means for every $1 liability, there must be $2 assets available to pay it when the cash is received.

$$\textbf{Current Ratio} \quad = \quad \frac{\text{Current Assets}}{\text{Current Liaibilities}}$$

Which is to be maintained in the ratio of:

Current Assets (2): Current Liabilities (1)

The quick ratio includes all the current assets, excluding inventory, divided by the current liabilities. The ratio between them can range from 1.3 to 1.5 against $1 of liability. These ratio values are considered as optimum amounts for them to be reported on. However, the real analysis of these ratios should be explained.

The working capital cycle gives a lot of info regarding when the cash will be received. Stated differently, all the assets such as inventory and accounts receivable are turned into cash. The main goal of the business is to earn cash – and do it fast. Since many costs are used in inventory manufacturing, the accounts payable stands in the liabilities, which must be paid quickly.

The working capital cycle is calculated with the average number of days inventory over a year, plus the average time taken for customers to pay. Then the average number of days for you to pay your suppliers is deducted.

Working capital cycle = avg. # in inventory number + avg. # A/R – avg. # of days to pay.

The average number of inventory days is calculated when we divide the total inventory by cost of sales and then multiplied by 365. The average number of days customers pay is when we divide total accounts receivables by total revenue and multiply it by 365 days. The average number of days to pay is calculated when we divide accounts payable with the credit purchases and multiply it by 365.

Let's assume the values are 80, 30, and 120, respectively, meaning that it takes an average of 120 days before customers pay, so the company takes loans to survive and pay other necessary costs. This makes cash flow look bad, as the business's cash suffers from poor cash flow – sometimes causing late payments, as well. This increases finance costs, which justifies the business's increased costs in the previous example (basic overview section). The business holds its inventory for a longer time and takes even longer to receive payments to make even more late payments to the suppliers.

This example clearly shows that the business is not doing well and must shut down its operations because it will lose the supplier's trust; it needs better inventory management – and an even better *cash recovery system.*

Let's say that these average days are 30, 10, and 7. This means that the company is paying for costs before the cash was received from the customers. On average, it has a full reserve of another 33 days; clearly, an abundant cash reserve is present with the business. It can easily make payments to vendors while maintaining enough cash to sustain operations for another three years. This raises another question regarding the business's use of cash. When there is an abundant amount of cash present in hand, the business must invest the excessive amount. Cash present in excess shouldn't be kept with the business for long as it won't provide value. Hence, the business must invest the additional amount in various instruments and other assets.

From the above illustration, you have a complete idea regarding how complex financial analysis can become. There are more financial analysis techniques, but they can become complex; this basic understanding is all you need for now.

Chapter 10: Closing Your Books

In the section, we will go over a few of the period-end closing techniques involving:

- Book closure event
- Some preliminary tasks to be done before the books closure event
- Adjusting the affected accounts
- Post book closure events

Let's get started!

Book Closure: What Is It and Why Is It Done?

Book closure (or "closing the book") is when all income/revenue events stop for the period – usually, year-end when owners wish to see the business's performance and affairs. Another instance might be when new federal regulations are announced, or a new budget is applicable.

At this time, books are finalized before being closed to ensure that an accurate picture of the company's financial health is depicted.

Crucial Preliminary Tasks Before You Can Close Your Books

Book closures don't occur instantly; some accounts must be prepared before closing. For instance, revenue and expense accounts are two significant areas requiring attention before being closed and reported. We focus more on the revenue and expense accounts because these accounts have certain events that recur over time, are easily traced, and must be accounted for.

For example, in administrative expenses, one of the most significant expenses is the salary and payroll; all the payments must be made before closing. Since salaries are paid the month after period worked, if this expense is left undocumented, it can disrupt the next period's accounts, resulting in incorrect totals.

Another significant expense – often overlooked - is depreciation. Depreciation is the value that your asset will lose over time due to usage or the allocation of the depreciable amount over the useful life of non-current assets. From this brief definition, it is clear that depreciation must be logged at the end of each year, and this task completed before books are closed. Depreciation is charged on different non-current assets on a different valuation basis. If you are using the digital tools for accounting, you will find sub-programs that automatically detect and charge depreciation on the non-current assets after you approve it. Typically, QuickBooks offers automatic depreciation for assets.

Similarly, some revenues are also not logged at the period or year-end. This typically involves those revenues related to goods sold before the period end but recorded as sales *after* the period. This situation occurs less often in everyday practice, but you'll need to remember that the revenue, in this case, must be logged before the period end or year-end.

Finance costs and tax must also be calculated before the books are closed. In practice, taxation is calculated from post book closure, whereas the finance cost is logged and accounted for before the books are closed. Taxation is calculated later on due to pending changes in the reporting accounts, affecting the tax totals in different manners. The finance cost is always logged on as a payment to the financial institution, but it is never accrued at the year-end. Thus, calculation of the finance cost accrued is crucially performed to ensure that all the information is in line so the financial institutions can reconcile interest they received as income.

7 Steps to Book Closure

As mentioned earlier, the revenue and expense accounts are affected most during the book closure event. During this time, seven steps are followed in the same sequence as described.

1. Pass All the Journal Entries

The first step before closing the books of accounts is to pass the journal entries. By this time, you may have gone through the preliminary process of identifying which heads of accounts are left unadjusted. The first step is to pass all the journal entries, particularly those discussed previously, in the preliminary tasks.

Once the journal entries are passed in the system, it will automatically make sure that all the entries have been accounted for this particular event. Make sure that you also pass the journal entries for any significant estimate. A significant estimate includes any provision for bad debts or provision of an event that occurred after the reporting date (this is just for reference to be used in the next series of the book).

2. Close All the Revenues and Expenses Accounts in the P/L Account

First, you will need to open a new account, which will be named the P/L account. Second, transfer all the revenue and expense account balances into the P/L account. This P/L account will clear the revenue and expense account balances and close them into the profit and loss ledger account. Third, make sure that no balance is left on any revenue or in any expense account. This includes the journal entries passed **(posted?)** during the process or accruals logged to adjust the balances.

At this stage, you can prepare a trial balance and have all the balances shifted in the trial balance. A better approach would be to clear out all the revenue and expense account balances and then make a trial balance. This will keep the trial account simple to understand, and you can see if all the revenues and the expenses have been accounted for.

3. Close the Balances of the Rest of the Ledgers

Now it is essential that you also close all the balances of other ledgers. For this, you will require no additional accounts. The ledgers remaining after closing revenue and expense accounts would be assets, liabilities, capital, and drawings. These accounts won't close for the year; instead, their balances will continue into the next period or year. That is why all the balance sheet elements, such as assets, liabilities, and owner's equity, have an opening balance. The same doesn't apply to profit and loss items, as they become part of another known as an *unappropriated* profit and loss account.

Once all the remaining account ledgers are closed, their balances are ready to be shifted in the trial balance. It means all the required entries in these ledgers have been passed, and after subtracting the debit side from the credit side of each ledger, a final closing balance becomes available to be shifted in the trial balance.

4. Prepare an Unadjusted Trial Balance

A trial balance is a statement that shows all the closing balances of every single ledger account. After combining the debit and the credit side of each ledger, the resulting trial becomes balanced. The sum of all the debit side accounts becomes equal to the credit side of the accounts. The trial balance also functions as the basis for the accounting equation and the ground foundation for the balance sheet or financial position statement.

An unadjusted trial balance is one in which the journal entries have not been accounted for yet. This includes adjustments to be made by the auditors. In companies, the trial balance is left unadjusted for auditors' adjustments because the auditor will pass some entries to ensure that the accounts represent the true and fair view. Thus, the trial balance is considered an unadjusted trial balance because some transactions are left pending for finalization later.

Once the ledger account closing balances have been taken, they are shifted into the trial balance, where they are checked for the omission, transposition, principle, and other errors. These errors will be explained later.

5. Include the Adjusted Journal Entries

The next step is to include all the adjusting journal entries. These journal entries will include those entries which the auditor might find or any other entry you find missed when the books were closed.

The actual area which the adjusted journal entries target is the post book closing entries, which relate to subsequent events. Subsequent events are those which occur after the closing date but relate to the year being reported. In cases like these, you must assess whether the event must be disclosed or accounted for in the financial statements. Sometimes, events like these appear; for instance, you are closing your books on 31st December 2xxx, and you realize after closing your books that most stocks you invested in are worth ¾ of what you invested initially, meaning you suffered a loss. Now you must disclose this information in your financial statements rather than accounting for it because you haven't sold these investments yet and hope to hold them for a little while longer.

Most of the time, the adjusting journal entries could be depreciation, impairment of assets, revaluation of assets, fair value valuation of stocks or property held as investments, etc. Other than depreciation, all these new accounting terms may seem surprising, but don't worry, these things will be explained later.

6. Prepare the Adjusted Trial Balance

Once again, the trial balance has to be made, but in this step, all the adjusting journal entries must be passed in the unadjusted trial balance, which will cause an adjusted trial balance. The adjusted trial balance doesn't mean it is the final trial balance, as it only contains the adjusting entries. There can be other entries, which will be passed before the accounts are closed.

The book closure date and the date when the financial statements are presented are two different dates. The book closure typically occurs within the one-month time frame after the period end date. In contrast, the business owners decide the reporting date when they wish to be presented with the management accounts (if someone else prepares your business accounts).

7. Generate Financial Statements

The final step is preparing the financial statements, which have been explained in the earlier chapters. These statements will include profit and loss statements, balance sheet, statement of cash flow, and changes in the owner's equity.

Use Digital Accounting Tools to Close the Books

All the steps mentioned before were done to show you how the accounts are closed manually clear*ly*. With the digital accounting software tools, all this is possible with just a button click. Almost every accounting software has a built-in function to close the books. Sometimes, software programs automatically generate reports without closing the books, whereas sometimes they close a particular range while generating reports.

Every accounting software has a period-change or a period-close wizard that performs the book closure on its own. However, the software doesn't close all the accounts' aspects because it can't detect unrecorded occurred events. Therefore, passing the journal entries and preparing the adjusted trial balance will be a task you must perform; otherwise, the software will close the period and close all the balances of revenues and expenses in the owner's equity. Once this is done, it becomes nearly impossible to reopen and pass the adjusting entry later on.

Thus, you should prepare a list of adjusting entries that are left unrecorded or might need amendments. This way, you can fix all the issues or problems later on when reconciling all the work in the end.

Chapter 11: Small Business Budgeting

In this chapter, we will discuss the fundamentals of budgeting. Along with that, we will also discuss:

- Secrets of a successful business
- The powerful tools for budgeting
- The expert view on how to perform budgeting

Budgeting: Secrets to a Successful Business

Most people plan out what they will do in life. Some even have elaborate and creating timing for defined goals they want to achieve. Meeting goals is dependent upon one's motivation to achieve more in the available time given. Our lives are full of examples where we plan out and execute decisions. In a certain way, we all try to plan, organize, and work on things we want to achieve.

Budgeting is a combination of multiple elements involving:

- Planning your goals and targeting time needed
- Organizing your schedule to accommodate steps needed to reach targets

- Availability and allocation of necessary resources to ensure that targets can be reached
- Estimating what percentage of the goal has been achieved

In management studies, budgeting plays a vital role in understanding the business's potential to grow. Budgets work as fertilizers for growing business because the budget layout can define how effectively and efficiently you reach targets and, ultimately, the goal.

These estimations and budgets can't be created by just one person, especially if it is a large entity. The involvement of multiple people from different operations creates a diversified viewpoint in terms of goal-reaching. Let's look at the steps involved in creating a budget.

1. SWOT Analysis or Market Analysis

Different types of market analysis are performed before the budgets are made regarding the business's principal activities. There are specific objectives to these analyses.

a. Understanding the Market

Understanding the market demand regarding the product requires you to estimate it first. This research can be difficult because of the data collection requirement, which include:

- Determining which geographical areas in which the products are sold
- Determining the total number of sales for a similar type of product being supplied in the whole market
- Determining the total market demand present throughout the year
- Learning seasonal demand increases within a year
- Discovering, on average, which product people prefer - and why

This requires immense effort and won't be easy!

b. Analyzing the Opportunities

Once the data is collected regarding the market, it has to meet the next objective: analyzing the opportunities. This task is aimed explicitly at understanding weak areas or qualities not yet introduced into the market.

c. The Potential Threats that can Hinder Growth

Once you understand the opportunities, it is crucial to understand which areas of your business are exposed to threats; you must analyze all the competitors present in the market and how much market share they currently hold.

Once these objectives are met, the SWOT Analysis (Strength, Weakness, Opportunities, and Threat Analysis) can be viewed as a whole regarding how the business can increase its total revenue in the next year. This entire analysis lays the foundation to decide:

- The goal for percentage increase in total revenue for the next year
- The total revenue limit the business can achieve in the next year
- The costs to be incurred to ii, above
- The optimal selling price per unit set for the next year

2. The Internal Procedures Analysis

Even though SWOT Analysis requires that the business's strengths and weaknesses are understood, the reality of whether this can be achieved or not is viewed through internal procedure analysis. This typically involves how much demand can be met with the current sales target. In simpler words: how many units can be manufactured? This involves an extensive understanding of what type of procedures would help achieve this target, the additional costs to bear to achieve this target, and the change in methods to ensure optimized costs.

This, in turn, produces answers regarding:

- The number of units that can be produced by the end of next year
- The production unit limits for the next year
- The additional or incremental costs to achieve the new production limit in the next year
- How costs can stay optimized while reaching a balanced supply limit

3. The Cash Flow Forecasts

Another crucial element of budgeting in the business involves the cash flow forecast. In this, the accounts and the recovery department both decide on how cash recovery can be made faster and optimal. Not only that, but they also plan how much cash they will receive from the customers and how long it will take them to pay their suppliers. These forecasts help the finance department understand where cash can be spent optimally while allowing them to look for areas where unnecessary costs can be cut.

This also involves the additional cost or machinery the production department may need to ensure that the production limit is optimally met. To achieve this, the cash flow forecast also involves bank loans or other forms of loans to be used to meet the cash demand while ensuring that costs associated with those finance are minimal or optimal.

4. Compile Everything for the Budget

After these analyses are performed, the budgets are set to reflect the increase in profits in the next year. The reports received from each type of analysis now allows the levels at which the costs will be optimized while ensuring higher profits in the coming year. The budget includes an entire forecast for the next year regarding every aspect of the business, allowing stakeholders to understand how the next year's targets can – and will - be met.

This process will create/generate the financial statements with the budgeted profit and loss statement, budgeted financial position statement, budgeted cash flow statements, and budgeted statement of equity changes. These financial statements shall be the final form, which will be presented as the conclusion of all the reports.

Once the reports and statements are finalized, every department or person is given a new set of targets they must achieve. They are also given the budget allocated to their heads for the next year.

As an entrepreneur, you will need to assess your budgets. These budgets are always estimates and simple forecasts, stating how the business will perform in the coming times. The key player in this entire process is the owner - doing his/her best to ensure that targets are met every month or quarter for the entire year.

Powerful Tools for Budgeting

Some powerful digital accounting tools perform extensive budget reports based on the information and transactions available for the current year. SAAP and other ERP software (Enterprise Resource Planning) provide projections for growth the business will achieve in the upcoming months. However, one limitation of these types of tools is that they cannot provide realistic opportunities that can be used for the business.

These tools can only compile the information or data given to them, but they cannot create out-of-the-limit reports, which can help you analyze the market status. You may want to save costs and prefer not to use such expensive tools. You can use templates and other forms of budgets that your accounting software will provide. This entire process was briefly explained so you can perform a small level of research and produce useful (and realistic) budgets for the future.

A fair recommendation is if you have a small business with a smaller operation like only one or two offices, use the pre-built templates of Microsoft office or the templates present in your digital accounting software. They can help in creating a valuable but small budget for your business. If, however, you must build a much more extensive budget, consult a more advanced book, or consult with an accountant to help you design the perfect budget and cash flow forecasts for your business.

Expert View Regarding Budgeting

Many experts believe that budgets are the only reason a business can survive in the market. Without the will or motivation for future growth, the future can look dim. The advice every expert accountant provides is that budgets define the organization itself. They also define whether the management or owners are serious about growing the business.

That said, many things affect any business's success; budgets are definitely an essential factor in terms of future growth!

Chapter 12: Three Small Business Accounting Pitfalls to Avoid

In this chapter, we will explain some of the common pitfalls small businesses face. These include the three significant downfalls.

1. Lost Receipts

One of the biggest and most common pitfalls of small businesses is losing receipts. Some business owners forget about the bills and receipts they have received because they are too busy managing other aspects of their work, making sure day-to-day operations are going smoothly.

The best way to manage this issue is by having an online app that takes images of the bills and receipts. Additionally, these apps remind you when you have an expense in the system for which there is no image of a receipt.

2. Poor Expense Tracking

Another major issue which the business owners face is not keeping a proper cash record. Cash is received and spent regularly, and there is rarely time to record where it comes from and where it goes.

The best way to manage this is by making cash vouchers whenever someone physically takes cash; this provides at least a temporary record to help reconcile the account later.

3. Failure to Monitor the Receivables and Payables

Another problem is the lack of records for receivables and payables. The issue is never in the payables (the other party, at some point, will receive their money), but rather, lies is when someone owes you money, and there's no record of the payment request.

The best way to tackle this issue is by keeping a steady record of the receivables and payables, ensuring your cash flow isn't disturbed at any point.

Conclusion

This book has not limited its scope to only the core fundamental ideas of accounting; we've provided the various ways you can easily use digital accounting tools and software to manage your records and financial transactions.

We've shown how you can use the various accounting tricks, management techniques, and semi-advanced methods to keep your business operations working steadily and effectively. Even as a beginner, you can create your budgets and analyze your accounts to get a clear picture regarding your company's performances – and how any investor or accountant would view your business activities.

The book is primarily aimed at entrepreneurs and other small business owners who have trouble understanding the accounts' crucial elements, which third parties such as banks, financial institutions, and investors look at deeply. Not only that, but we have also shown that your operational work, such as payroll, tax, and other activities, can be easily managed with digital software and tools.

We hope you've found this book beneficial as you consider the best ways to account for revenue and expenses in your business!

Here's another book by Robert McCarthy that you might like

Appendix: Accounting Glossary

How often have you hung up the phone or left a meeting with your accountant far more confused than before? Most of that is down to not understanding the accounting terms, so below is a list of the most common terms, relevant abbreviations, and definitions.

Balance Sheet Terms

Balance sheets are at the top of the pack, the most common of the financial statements an accountant will produce. This section defines the common terms relating to the balance sheet.

Accounts Payable (AP) - The Accounts Payable includes all business expenses incurred but not paid. The AP account is always recorded on the balance sheet as a liability as it is a debt the company owes.

Accounts Receivable (AR) – The Accounts Receivable covers all sales provided by a company that haven't yet been paid for. The AR account is always recorded on the balance sheet as an asset likely to convert into cash shortly.

Accrued Expense (AE) – This is an expense incurred but not yet paid.

Asset (A) – An asset is anything of a monetary value owned by the company. Typically, they are listed in liquidity order, starting with the most liquid, which is cash and ending with the least liquid, such as land.

Balance Sheet (BS) – This is a financial statement listing all the company assets, liabilities, and equity. Its name suggests that it follows an equation – Assets = Liabilities + Equity.

Book Value (BV) – Every asset loses value over time, and this is called depreciation. The Book Value indicates the original value minus any depreciation accrued over time.

Equity (E) – Equity indicates any value left after the removal of liabilities. Going back to the balance sheet equation of Assets + Liabilities + Equity, if you deduct liabilities from assets, the remainder is the equity. This is the part of the company owned by the company owners and investors.

Inventory (I) – This term is used to classify assets purchased by a company to sell on to customers but remain unsold. The inventory account decreases every time an asset is sold to a customer.

Liability (L) – Every debt owned by a company and not yet paid are Liabilities. The most common liabilities include loans, payroll, and Accounts Payable.

Income Statement Terms

The second most common financial statement is the Income Statement, more commonly known as the Profit and Loss Statement. These are the most common terms that relate to it:

Capital (CAP) – This is an asset (financial) or its value, for example, cash. To calculate working capital, you subtract your current liabilities from the current assets – this provides the assets or cash the company has to work with.

Cost of Goods Sold (COGS) – These are the expenses related directly to creating a service or product but, what you won't find here are the business's running costs. Common examples include Direct Labor or Materials in providing goods or services.

Depreciation (DEP) – This is the term used to account for an asset's loss in value over a period. Depreciation can only be warranted on assets with substantial values, and the most common assets are equipment and vehicles. Depreciation is shown as an expense on the Income Statement, normally under the category of Non-Cash Expense. This is because it has no direct impact on the cash position of the company.

Expense (Cost) – Expenses are fees a company incurs and are split into variable, fixed, operational, or accrued costs incurred through a business operation:

- **Variable Expenses (VE)** – expenses such as labor, or any expense that can change within a given period
- **Fixed Expenses (FE)** – payments such as rent that are paid regularly
- **Operational Expenses (OE)** – business expenses that do not relate directly to producing services or goods, such as advertising, insurance, property taxes, etc.
- **Accrued Expenses (AE)** – expenses incurred and not yet paid

Gross Margin (GM) – The Gross Margin is calculated by dividing Gross Profit by Revenue. It shows how profitable, or otherwise, a company is once the Cost of Goods Sold is deducted.

Gross Profit (GP) - This figure indicates whether a company is profitable before taking overheads into account. GP is calculated by deducting the Cost of Goods Sold from Revenue.

Income Statement (Profit and Loss – IS or P&L) – often called the P&L or Profit and Loss Account, it is a financial statement showing expenses, revenue, and profits over a period. Earned revenue is displayed at the top, and expenses are all deducted – the final figure is the Net Income.

Net Income (NI) – This is the amount of profit earned, calculated by subtracting all expenses from each period's revenue. This includes COGS, taxes, depreciation, and overhead.

Net Margin (NM) – This percentage shows a company's profit related to revenue. The calculation is done by dividing Net Income by Revenue for the specified period.

Revenue (Sales or Rev) – Any money a business earns.

General Terms

Lastly are the terms that bear no relation to any specific statement, the general accounting terms.

401k/ROTH 401K – This is a type of savings where employees can put some of their salaries into a retirement account based on the investment. The money is usually tax-free until withdrawn, but employees can continue contributing to their 401K after taxes. Some employers may also match their employee contributions but only to a specified percentage.

Accounting Period – This is designated in every financial statement, including the Income Statements, Statement of Cash Flow, and the Balance Sheet. The period indicates the time reported in each statement.

Accounting Equation – Double-entry bookkeeping that uses the accounting equation of Assets = Liabilities + Owner's Equity or a longer version of it – Assets + Expenses = Liabilities + Owner's Equity + Revenue.

Accrual Accounting – This method of accounting is where income and expenditure is recorded as they are incurred, not at the time they are paid. For example, Sam purchases a book in November but doesn't pay the bill until December. The purchases are shown in the Income Statement in the accounts as being made in November, not in December when the bill was paid.

Allocation – This describes how funds are assigned to each period or account. For instance, costs can be allocated over several months, such as insurance payments or several departments, such as admin costs for companies with several departments.

Business Entity – Often called the Legal Entity, this indicates the type or structure of a business. Some of the more common entities include Partnership, Sole Proprietor, LLC (Limited Liability Corp). C-Corp, and S-Corp. Every entity comes with its own set of tax implications, laws, and requirements.

Cash Accounting – This method of accounting records income and expenditure at the time they are paid, not at the time they were incurred. For example, Sam buys his book in November and paus the bill in January. The income statement will show the purchase as being made in December, when it was paid for.

Cash Book – This is the book where funds are recorded as they move in and out of the company through the company bank account. Every transaction in the cash book should show the following information:

- Transaction date
- Transaction amount
- Description
- The relevant bookkeeping accounts

Cash Flow (CF) – This is the term used to describe cash flowing in and out of a company. Net Cash Flow is determined by subtracting the Ending Cash Balance from the Beginning Cash Balance. If it is a positive number, it shows more cash has flowed into the business than out of it, whereas if it is a negative number, it indicates more cash has gone out than in.

Contra – When a payment is made to an account in the bookkeeping system, and the same payment is then made back out of the account, it is known as a contra. This means they cancel one another out, for example, $300 paid to the Sales account, but the bookkeeper realizes it should have been paid to a different account and pays it back out. Thus, the two payments cancel each other out.

Conversion Balances – When the bookkeeping records are transferred between two different accounting software, it is known as conversion. The closing balance is taken from the original software and entered as the new software's opening balance.

Certified Public Accountant (CPA) – This is a professional designation earned by an accountant after passing a CPA exam. They must also fulfill a set of requirements for work experience and education; these are different in each State.

Credit – Credits are listed on the right side of the double-entry accounting method. Credit entries decrease expenses and assets and increase equity, liabilities, and income. Any money owed by the business to vendors or suppliers is shown as a credit, along with any money owed on credit cards or bank loans.

Credit Entry (CR) – credit entry

Debit – Debits are listed on the left side of the double-entry accounting method. A debit increases expenses and assets and decreases equity, liabilities, and income.

Debit Record (DR) – debit entry

Deductible – This is a purchase a business may claim as a business expense because it reduces the profit. In turn, it reduces how much income tax the business owes the government. Non-deductible purchases are those that cannot reduce the tax and profit, i.e., when the business owner purchases personal items with business funds.

Diversification – This is a common method used to reduce risk by allocating capital across several assets, ensuring one asset's performance doesn't impact the total performance.

Double-Entry – This is an accounting method where every transaction is inputted twice – as both a credit and a debit. The total debits must be equal to the total credits; if not, it is not balanced, and the error needs to be found and corrected.

Drawings – Any money a business owner withdraws from the business for their own personal use.

Enrolled Agent (EA) – This is a professional designation assigned to those who have passed tests in personal and business expertise. Typically, they complete tax filings for businesses to ensure IRS compliance.

Financial Statements – These are reports the accountant produces when the financial year ends. These are based on the financial data the bookkeeper has entered into the system and they show whether a business is making a profit or not. They also show what the business is worth and are used for calculating taxes due to the government, i.e. income tax.

Fixed Cost (FC) – This is a cost that won't change as the volume of sales changes. An example of this is salaries or rent, which do not change when a company sells more or less. A Variable Cost is the opposite of this.

General Ledger (GL) – This shows the entire record of financial transactions for a company. It is usually used to help prepare the financial statements.

Generally Accepted Accounting Principles (GAAP) – These are the rules all accountants must abide by when doing any accounting. The rules were established to ensure an easy comparison of "apples to apples" when going over their clients' financial accounts.

Individual Retirement Account (IRA or ROTH IRA) – These are retirement savings. Traditional IRAs allow an individual to place pre-tax dollars into investments that can be grown "tax-deferred." This means that any dividend income or capital gains are not taxed until the money is withdrawn. In most cases, it is also tax-deductible. A ROTH IRA is not, but some distributions are tax free and not taxable when withdrawn.

Insolvency – the definition of insolvency is "a state where an individual or organization cannot meet their financial obligations with lenders when payments come due."

Interest – This is when a company pays on a line of credit, loan, or mortgage, over and above the principal balance repayment.

Journal Entry (JE) – These are how changes and updates are made to the books. Each entry must have its identifier, the date, an amount, a debit/credit, and a code showing which account has been changed.

Limited Liability Company (LLC) – This is a corporate structure in which each member cannot be held personally accountable for the liabilities or debts a company has. This shields the owners from losing everything if the company were to be sued.

Liquidity – This is a term that references the speed at which an asset can be turned into cash. Stocks have more liquidity than buildings because they can be sold much quicker.

Material – This term is used to refer to whether decisions are influenced by information. For example, if a company has millions of dollars in revenue, a couple of dollars is not material. GAAP dictates that every material consideration is disclosed.

On Credit/On Account – When a purchase is made on these terms, it indicates the payment will be made in time, but the customer takes the product straight away.

Overhead – These are the business-related expenses but only for running the company – they do not include expenses related to making a product or delivering a service, but they include salaries and rent.

Payroll – This account shows all payments made to employees as salaries or wages, bonuses, and any deductions. Shown as a liability on the balance sheet if there are unpaid wages or vacation pay that has accrued.

PAYE – Pay As You Earn, or PAYE is where individuals who earn a salary or a wage has tax deducted at source by their employer. This deduction must then be passed on by the employer to the government, typically monthly.

Petty Cash – Most businesses keep an amount of cash on the premises for small purchases, such as stamps, stationery, etc. This is kept in a safe place, and the bookkeeper must monitor it carefully. The petty cash book contains records of all monies paid out, and this is then included in the accounts. When the money gets low, more money can be given to top it up.

Present Value (PV) – This term indicates the value an asset has on a given day. It is based on a theory that says something is more valuable today than tomorrow because of inflation.

Receipts – This is a document showing payment has been made for something. Businesses produce receipts when they provide a service or product and receive receipts when they pay for a service or other businesses' goods. Received receipts must always be saved so a company can prove the accuracy of its incurred expenses.

Reconcile - This is a process whereby one set of documents or figures must be matched to another. For example, the cash book should be matched to the bank account, and any differences should be investigated and fixed. Another example is ensuring that all the invoices shown on a supplier statement have been received and requesting any that are missing.

Return on Investment (ROI) – This term refers to the profit (return) that a company made on investments. These days, it is a little looser and includes returns on other objectives and projects. For example, a company spent $1500 on marketing and received $3000 in profit. The ROI on what was spent on marketing could be stated as 50%.

Single-Entry - This bookkeeping method is where the financial transactions are entered once, usually within a cash book system. Ledgers and journals are not used for the balancing process.

Trial Balance (TB) - The Trial Balance lists all of the general ledger accounts and their balances, either credit or debit. The total debits must be equal to the total credits, so it is called a balance.

Variable Cost (VC) - Variable costs change as the sales volume changes, and they are opposite to Fixed Costs. They increase as the sales increase because they are expenses related to delivering a sale. For example, a company sells many products and needs to purchase more raw materials to meet demand.

Write-off - If a customer does not pay an amount due, sometimes it can be written off. This entails an entry in the accounts to zero the customer account.

Year-End - This indicates the financial year end and is one of the busiest times of year for a bookkeeper. All the yearly accounts must be finalized and given to the accountant to work out what taxes need to be paid.

Those are the most common terms related to accounting, those you are most likely to come across frequently.

References

Chapter 1: What is Accounting (and Can I Do It on My Own)?

What is an Accountant, and what do they do? By: daveramsey.com https://www.daveramsey.com/blog/what-is-an-accountant

Why and How to Be Your Own Accountant- The Tools to Use and The Benefits You will See. By author: Scott Morris https://skillcrush.com/blog/be-your-own-accountant/

Can I Be My Own Accountant? By: Paypath.com https://www.paypath.com/Financial-Resources/can-i-be-my-own-accountant

Chapter 2: Accounting vs. Bookkeeping

Accounting and Bookkeeping. By: toppr.com https://www.toppr.com/guides/accounting-and-auditing/theoretical-framework-of-accounting/bookkeeping-2/

Accountant vs. Bookkeeper. By: On-Core Bookkeeping https://www.youtube.com/watch?v=XsMvh4Ygv9I

Top 8 Differences Between Bookkeeping And Accounting. By: flatworldsolutions.com https://www.flatworldsolutions.com/financial-services/differences-between-bookkeeping-accounting.php

Chapter 3: Which Accounting Methods Suits My Small Business?

Double Entry Vs. Single Entry Accounting|, which One is Best! By author: Yaqub Nipu

https://onlineaccountinghub.com/double-entry-vs-single-entry/

Best Accounting Methods for Small Business. By author: Billie Anne Grigg

https://www.fundera.com/blog/accounting-methods-for-small-business

Cash vs. Accrual Accounting: What's best for your small business? By QuickBooks

https://quickbooks.intuit.com/r/bookkeeping/cash-vs-accrual-accounting-whats-best-small-business/

Chapter 4: 10 Tools for Digital Accounting

12 Accounting Tools Every Small Business Needs. By author: Ben Rashkovich

https://www.fundera.com/blog/accounting-tools

The Best Small Business Accounting Software for 2020. By author: Kathy Yakal

https://www.pcmag.com/picks/the-best-small-business-accounting-software

Chapter 5: Setting Up the Chart of Accounts

Accounting For Beginners #20 / Chart of Accounts / Assets, Liabilities, Equity, Revenues, Expenses. By: CPA Strength
https://www.youtube.com/watch?v=yXJVISZA8yU

Develop a Chart of Accounts for Your Small Business. By author: Rosemary Carlson https://www.thebalancesmb.com/develop-the-chart-of-accounts-for-your-small-business-392997

Chart of Accounts- Explanation. By author: Harold Averkamp (Site: accountingcoach.com) https://www.accountingcoach.com/chart-of-accounts/explanation/2

Chapter 6: Transactions, Ledger and Journals

Ledger Account Definition, Format, Types, and Example. By: toppr.com

https://www.toppr.com/guides/fundamentals-of-accounting/books-of-prime-entry/ledger-accounts/

Chapter 7: Payroll, Processing, and Taxes

How to do Payroll Taxes and Process Payroll Yourself. By squareup.com

https://squareup.com/us/en/townsquare/how-to-do-payroll-yourself

Chapter 11: Small Business Budgeting

A Guide to Successful Small Business Budget Planning. By author: Sonya Stinson (Site:

Nationalfunding.com) https://www.nationalfunding.com/blog/small-business-budget-planning/

Made in the USA
Las Vegas, NV
19 July 2024

92626629R00140